THE TEACH YOURSELF BOOKS

FISHING

**Uniform with this volume
and in the same series**

Teach Yourself Archery
Teach Yourself Athletics
Teach Yourself Badminton
Teach Yourself Billiards and Snooker
Teach Yourself Bowls
Teach Yourself Cricket
Teach Yourself Cycling
Teach Yourself Fencing
Teach Yourself Fly Fishing
Teach Yourself Golf
Teach Yourself Hockey
Teach Yourself Horse Management
Teach Yourself: Indoor Aquaria
Teach Yourself Judo
Teach Yourself Karate
Teach Yourself Lawn Tennis
Teach Yourself Mountain Climbing
Teach Yourself Physical Fitness
Teach Yourself Rugby Football
Teach Yourself Sailing
Teach Yourself Skiing
Teach Yourself Soccer
Teach Yourself Swimming
Teach Yourself Table Tennis
Teach Yourself Underwater Swimming

TEACH YOURSELF
FISHING

By

TOM RODWAY

TEACH YOURSELF BOOKS
ST. PAUL'S HOUSE   WARWICK LANE
LONDON EC4

First Edition . . *1950*
This Impression . . *1969*

All rights reserved. No part of this publication may be reproduced or transmitted in any form or by any means, electronic or mechanical, including photocopy, recording, or any information storage and retrieval system, without permission in writing from the publisher.

SBN 340 05585 5

Printed in Great Britain for The English Universities Press Ltd., London by Elliott Bros. & Yeoman, Ltd., Liverpool

CONTENTS

PART I

SOMETHING ABOUT FISH

Chap.		Page
I	Something About Fish	3

PART II

COARSE FISHING

II	Coarse Fishing—Equipment	13
III	Where to Fish	23
IV	Coarse Fishing—Float Fishing Methods: Legering and Float Legering; Paternostering; Free Lining; Spinning; Fly-Fishing	27
V	Pike—Equipment	60
VI	Coarse Fishing—Spinning for Pike	69
VII	Live-Baiting	76

PART III

SEA FISHING

VIII	Sea Fishing—Equipment	83
IX	Sea Fishing—Shore Fishing	90
X	Sea Fishing—Fly-Fishing and Spinning	100
XI	Sea Fishing—Boat Fishing	107
XII	Sea Fishing—Big Game	115

PART IV

TROUT, SALMON AND SEA-TROUT FISHING

CHAP.		PAGE
XIII	Fly-Fishing—General	121
XIV	Wet Fly-Fishing for Trout	136
XV	Loch Fishing for Trout	145
XVI	Dry Fly Trout Fishing	149
XVII	Trout Fishing—Other Methods	157
XVIII	Worm-Fishing for Trout	161
XIX	Salmon Fishing	164
XX	Greased-Line Fishing	175
XXI	Spinning for Salmon	180
XXII	Worming for Salmon	189
XXIII	Sea-Trout Fishing	192
XXIV	Knots and Oddments	198
XXV	Fishing Etiquette	202

PREFACE

"TEACH YOURSELF FISHING"—it will be agreed that it is pure presumption on the part of an author to attempt to encompass in one small volume all that is implied by this title. There is, however, a loophole for excuse. "Teaching yourself" is the only way you will ever learn to fish. You may acquire from others the elements of the technique, the essentials of tackle requirements, even where and how to set about fishing. But to become a fisherman you alone, through practise, can teach yourself the art. This book tries to put your feet on the first steps of the ladder.

And it is well worthwhile. True "pools" and "lines", "doubles" and "trebles" cannot in this pastime make you rich overnight. True, the only reward for many hours of patient fishing may sometimes be but the littlest fish.

The real gain is elsewhere. Fishing is an adventure into another world, a water world, a world in which politics, business, domestic strife, international relations and all the host of everyday worries of modern man have no place. It is, if you will, an escape—from fantasy into reality. The true fisherman is a member of a brotherhood bound together by a common philosophy which has its roots in the earliest beginnings of civilised man.

And when all is said and done the hours spent in this pastime are not wasted. I have a strong suspicion that the pearly gates have been opened to more than one whose only claim to admittance was his ability to say "I, too, was a fisherman".

PART I

SOMETHING ABOUT FISH

Chapter 1

SOMETHING ABOUT FISH

If you are going to take up fishing as a hobby it seems natural that you should want to know something about the creatures which, for the rest of your life (I have never heard of anyone who, once a fisherman, has given it up), you are going to study and try to catch. We have all seen fish, plenty of them, and it is quite evident that they all share certain fairly easily recognisable characteristics. They are not, for instance, the possessors of arms and legs, but have fins and a well-developed tail instead. Most are covered with scales and are slimy to the touch. They have eyes and what appears to be a nose, but no visible ears: and all those that are not " shell-fish " have a bony skeleton of some sort.

It so happens that the skeleton of all fish are not of the same kind. The " class " of fish is divided into two main sub-classes, fish having a true bony skeleton and fish having a cartilaginous skeleton. Of the latter class the sharks, topes, rays and dogfish are the only ones likely to be of interest to the fisherman.

The remainder are true " bony fishes " and are divided into *orders* (about thirty in number), which in turn are made up of the *families* consisting of groups of *genera*. Each *genus*, in turn, is composed of a number of *species* of fish.

Thus the trout, for example, would have a family tree something of this sort.

Species	..	Trout	.. (Salmo Trutta)
Genus	..	Salmo	.. (First cousin to the salmon, etc.)
Family	..	Salmonidæ	.. (Related to other genera such as the onchorynchus or Pacific Salmon, etc.)

Sub-Order..	Salmonoidea..	(Contains other allied families [such as smelts).
Order ..	Isospondyli ..	(All fish with the swim bladder connected to the gullet by a duct belong to this, i.e. herring family or Clupei-[oidea).
Sub-Class..	Neoptergii ..	(Literally "modern finned", actually all fish that breathe
Class ..	Pisces ..	Fish. [with gills only).

This perhaps all looks rather alarming and technical, and I think Mr. Chapman Pincher, in that quite excellent *A Study of Fishes*, has on page 14, put the matter much more understandably and without the bother of Latin names. I will quote this table in full for it shows very clearly where every species fits in (see diagram A on page 6).

From the fisherman's point of view, however, it is probably more important to classify our fish somewhat differently. We want to know how and where to fish for each species. With this in view we can make a family tree of our own (see diagram B on page 7).

The slimy covering of a fish is exuded for a definite purpose. It helps to overcome the frictional drag on the water when the fish is swimming, and it also helps to keep the fish "waterproof". A freshwater fish which has had a large part of its natural slime removed tends to "leak" water into its muscle, and becomes literally waterlogged. This is why you should handle all fish which are not of sufficient size to keep with great care.

The scales help also in preventing the entry of water into the tissues. The loss of a patch of scales due to careless handling may well lead to death.

All the fish we are interested in breathe by means of gills. These are merely very thin-walled blood vessels which allow an exchange through the walls between those gases dissolved in the liquid blood on the inside and those in the water on the outside. It is through the gills that the fish derives oxygen and rids itself of waste products, such as carbon dioxide. Any damage to a fish's gills may cause death. The smallest puncture in a gill filament inevitably means that the fish will bleed to death. Bear this in mind when removing the hook from little fishes.

Respiration is, with little doubt, the main problem facing all freshwater and many marine fishes. As a land vertebrate you encounter an entirely different set of difficulties. Gravity and loss of heat are the land animal's main enemies. A given size and weight of creature requires a specially constructed skeleton suitable to support him. Even so, falling any distance means disaster. Animals, too, must eat far more than is required for energy of movement and growth simply in order to supply fuel for maintaining bodily warmth. But they breathe an air fairly constant in its proportions of oxygen and which is able to absorb a limitless amount of the carbon dioxide which is exhaled.

To a fish gravity obviously holds no dangers. Being cold-blooded, i.e. keeping his body temperature always about the same as his surroundings, the problem of heat conservation is non-existent. All the food he eats can be devoted to energy for movement and for growth. He has a skeleton which does not " set " and which has no weight to support, and on these grounds there is no limit to his size. But for any species the proportion of gill area to body surface is always constant. But his weight increases roughly as the cube of his linear dimensions, while his surface, and therefore his gill area, increases only as the square of these dimensions. This means that the bigger the fish grows the less gill surface he has to effect the necessary exchange of gases required by each pound of body weight. When we add to this the fact that the amount of dissolved oxygen in water (this is the only oxygen available to the fish, the " O " in H_2O is in chemical combination and is not available) may be at one moment in the twenty-four hours as much as 10 c.c. per litre and at another as little as 3 c.c., it becomes evident that the problem of acquiring sufficient oxygen for bodily functions becomes very acute at times. Much of the fish's behaviour is bound up with the changes in the oxygen content of the water in which he lives.

All fish have ears, but while they have no external opening, they are none the less built on the same lines as yours and are very receptive to even small noises.

TEACH YOURSELF FISHING

A

LIVING FISHES

With jaws — **Without jaws** Lampreys and Hagfishes

With jaws branches into:

- **Skeleton Cartilaginous** — Sharks, Dogfish, Rays, Skate, Rabbit fishes
- **Skeleton Bony**

Skeleton Bony branches into:

- **Breathing by "Lungs" and Gills** — **Lung Fishes**
- **Breathing by Gills only**

Breathing by Gills only branches into:

- **Pectoral Fin with a Bony Lobe at the Base** — **Birchir**
- **Pectoral Fin with no Basal Lobe**

Pectoral Fin with no Basal Lobe branches into:

- **Scales Ganoid** — Sturgeons, Gar Pike
- **Scales not Ganoid**

Scales not Ganoid branches into:

- **Gills Tuft-like** — **Sea Horses, Pipe Fishes**
- **Gills Comb-like**

Gills Comb-like branches into:

- **Fine Soft-rayed**
- **Fins with some Spiny Rays**

Fine Soft-rayed branches into:

Ventral Fins set well back
1. Catfishes
2. Eels, Morays, Conger
3. Herring, Whitefish, Salmon, Trout, Smelts, Grayling
4. Pikes, Mudminnows, Alaskan Blackfish
5. Carps, Breams, Barbel, Electric Eel, Roach, Rudd, Minnow, Tench

Ventral Fins set forward
1. Killifishes, Four-eyed Fish
2. Cod, Haddock, Whiting, Ling

Fins with some Spiny Rays
1. Perches, Red Mullet, Archer fish
2. Wrasses
3. John Dory
4. Stickleback, Scorpion fishes, Gurnards, Lumpsuckers
5. Mackerel, Tunny, Swordfish
6. Remora
7. Flat Fishes
8. Grey Mullets, Barracuda, Climbing Perch
9. Anglers, Frogfishes, Batfishes

SOMETHING ABOUT FISH

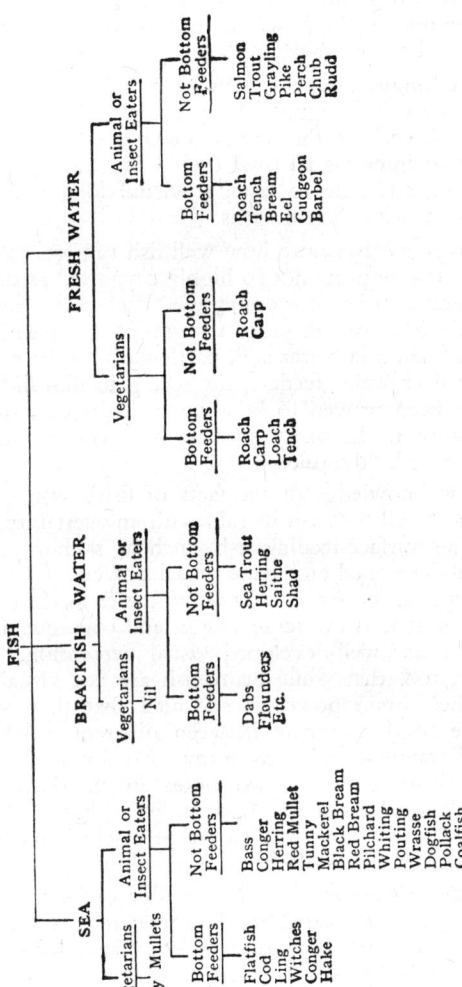

N.B.—Certain fish are shown in two or more classes, i.e. Roach. This is because they have at different times the attributes of each class.

The nostrils seen just above the mouth on most fishes are the external openings to the nose. Many fish rely largely on their sense of smell to find their food.

Fish also have tongues, but often the taste buds are not, as in man, confined to the tongue. Many fish have taste buds on special organs, such as the barbels of cod, etc. Others have taste buds at intervals all over their body. Many fish are thus aware of, and able to taste, foodstuff long before even they sample it with their mouths.

Much controversy exists as to how well fish can see. The fish's eye is in some respects not so highly organised as that of a land vertebrate. It has, for example, a somewhat primitive focusing device. But in other respects it is extremely well adapted for vision in water and, particularly in the case of the night or deep-water feeders, for seeing in dim light. Many fish have been proved to be able to distinguish one colour from another. In many species, however, colour-blindness appears to be the rule.

At present the knowledge of the facts of fish's vision is still in its infancy. All that can be said with any certainty is that some of the surface-feeding fish, such as salmon and trout, have well-developed and acute visual powers. Others endowed with special sense and taste organs, such as the cod or barbel, have less need for acute vision, and consequently have probably a less well-developed visual perception. It seems probable, too, that while many fish are not visually colour-blind, their brain power is so small that they are mentally unable to discriminate between different colours without special training, rather as many men do not consciously discriminate between two notes in the bottom octave of the piano unless they especially listen, but merely class them together as " low ". Fish are probably infinitely more susceptible to shade and tone than to colour.

How much the sensation of pain is capable of being felt by a fish is uncertain. Experiments show that most fish are virtually insensible to the type of pain associated by land vertebrates with injuries more or less severe. But, on the other hand, most fish show themselves to be extremely sensitive to change in pressure and temperature on the skin

SOMETHING ABOUT FISH

and exhibit extremes of discomfort, if not of actual pain, on being held, for instance, in a warm hand.

The alimentary canal in fishes follows the same pattern as that in other vertebrates. The gullet leads into the stomach, which in turn leads to the intestine, which is short or long according to the type of food eaten, and the waste is excreted at the vent. The fish has a liver, kidneys and most of the normal digestive organs and glands to be found in land animals. Marine bony fish drink copiously but excrete little urine, since water is required in their blood and body to replace that lost by osmosis through the gills. The sea fish faces the danger of drying out. The freshwater fish, however, faces the danger of becoming waterlogged. His blood and the contents of his body cells are more saline than the water he lives in and this water, consequently, is always seeping in through the cell walls. As a result the freshwater fish does not drink, but excretes large quantities of urine none the less.

All the fishes we are interested in, except the tope, shark and dogfish, reproduce themselves by means of eggs. This is a wasteful method even in the most careful species. Some indication of the number of eggs required to be laid to produce replacements for themselves by two parent fishes may be judged from the following examples of average-sized fish.

Conger	12 million
Herring	20,000
Perch	50,000
Pike	150,000
Trout	2,000
Carp	300,000

Few fish show any signs of parental care for their eggs or offspring. Exceptions, such as the genus Salmo, which build redds in which to lay their eggs, or the sticklebacks, which make a nest, are notable by their rarity.

All fish have fins. These are basically seven in number, and of these, three, the tail, the dorsal and the anal, are single fins, while the other four are arranged in two sets of pairs, the pectorals and the ventrals. While in certain fish some of the fins are adapted to special uses (such as the protective spines on the dorsal of the perch), the normal fish uses these fins for specific purposes. Thus the tail is used to provide power for swimming. The dorsal and anal fins are used as keels to maintain an upright position and direction while swimming, and the ventrals and pectorals are primarily used to regain vertical stability, to act as brakes both in stopping and turning, and to maintain position when stationary in slight currents.

The scales of fish are of considerable interest to anglers. Most fish are hatched out naked, but the scales start to form after a few weeks of life. The young fish forms a full complement of scales initially, and since this number must suffice to cover him both as a tiny alevin and as a full-grown specimen, it follows that each scale must grow with the fish. This it does, but in so doing it leaves written indelibly on itself a very exact record of the rate of growth of the fish. You can, for instance, remove a scale from a salmon and by examining it under a magnifying glass tell, not only its age, the number of years it has spent in fresh water and in the sea, and the number of times it has spawned, but also the exact length of the fish at any given moment in its life.

PART II

COARSE FISHING

Chapter II

COARSE FISHING

EQUIPMENT

BEFORE describing the various methods by which coarse fish may be captured, I think it would be as well if I gave a short list of the equipment required.

The minimum outfit is a rod, reel, line, float, hooks and sinker. You may even do without the float under certain circumstances; but whatever you do have, or do without, you must have "balance" in your tackle. It is impossible to handle with any degree of success or comfort a light rod fitted with a heavy reel. Something may perhaps be done with a light reel on a heavy rod; but even this can be considered only as a makeshift. The line also must be suited to the rod. A good rod can soon be spoilt by using a heavy line with it; in a short while the top develops a permanent droop and in this state refuses to respond with the speed necessary to connect with shyly biting fish.

The general coarse fish rod should be light, fairly stiff and at least twelve feet long. A short rod is an abomination when you find that you have to fish over a bed of weeds, or when you cannot get close to the water because of a stretch of boggy ground. In any case it is always advisable to keep as far away from the edge as is reasonably possible, so as to avoid alarming the fish. Most modern general-purpose rods are in three joints, with split bamboo tops, and measure about thirteen feet.

The reel should have a diameter of at least three inches and should be provided with a check, adjustable for preference. I prefer a reel made of metal. A really good reel is expensive—it will probably cost nearly as much as, or even more than, the rod; but it is worth it to have a thoroughly reliable article. There are many excellent designs in aluminium alloy, light in weight, fitted with large drums for quick winding, cage type to prevent fouling of the line, and with a special lever which enables the drum to run free whilst fishing a swim but which restores a pressure on the drum immediately the finger is taken from the lever and so prevents any over-running. There is also an arrangement which enables pressure on the drum to be adjusted to the extent required.

Lines present a very wide choice; but, if I were limited to one and that one had to be reasonably cheap, I should choose a line of dressed plaited flax with a breaking strain of about six pounds. Fifty yards of such a line will serve for almost any freshwater coarse fish with the exception of pike, and, if carefully dried after use, will last for years. Line driers can be bought, but a very good substitute is the back of a chair. When on a fishing holiday I always unwind my line round the back of a chair in my bedroom every night, and re-wind it again in the morning.

Floats are many and various. They are made of cork, celluloid, goose-quills, swan-quills, porcupine-quills and even varnished paper. For a start I would suggest one light celluloid or porcupine-quill float about four inches in length, one goose-quill of about seven inches, a small egg-float made of a porcupine-quill with a ball of cork about the size of a hazel nut, and a larger egg-float with a cork about an inch and a half long.

Hooks, with gut attachments, can be obtained in a great many sizes and shapes. For all-round work I would suggest a dozen each in sizes 2, 4, 6, 8, 10, 12 and 14, with round bends and a side twist. Gut casts are also required; but until one becomes thoroughly used to handling the rod and has had some experience in catching fish of, say, a pound to two pounds in weight, I should not recommend the use of any gut (or nylon) in sizes smaller than 4X. The very fine drawn gut, sizes 5X and 6X, require very delicate handling and only cause disappointments in the loss of good fish when used by anglers with a limited experience. Designs of hooks other than the round bend with side twist can be obtained and some are preferred with certain types of bait; but for all-round use and reliability in hooking my preference has always been for the type I have suggested.

COARSE FISHING

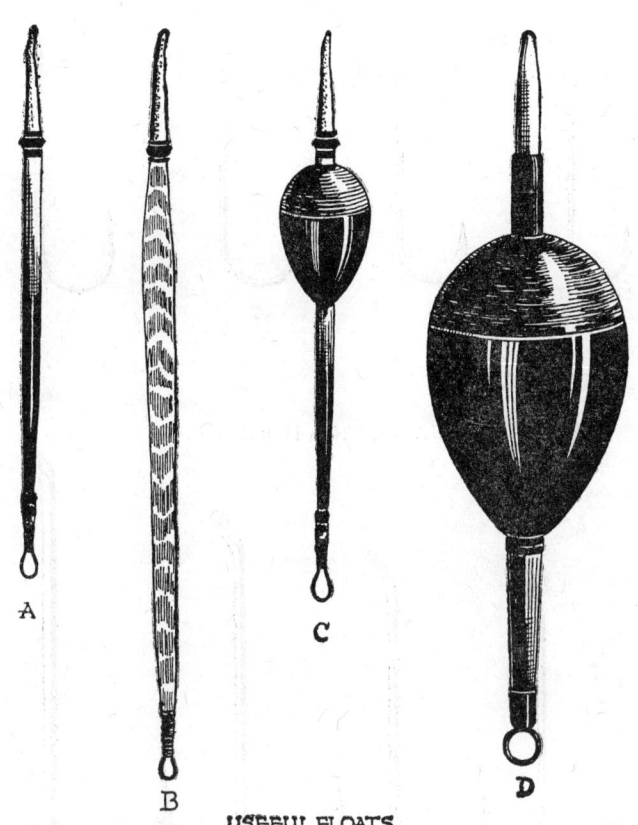

USEFUL FLOATS

- **A** – PORCUPINE
- **B** – GOOSE QUILL
- **C** – PORCUPINE WITH 'EGG' OF CORK
- **D** – EGG FLOAT

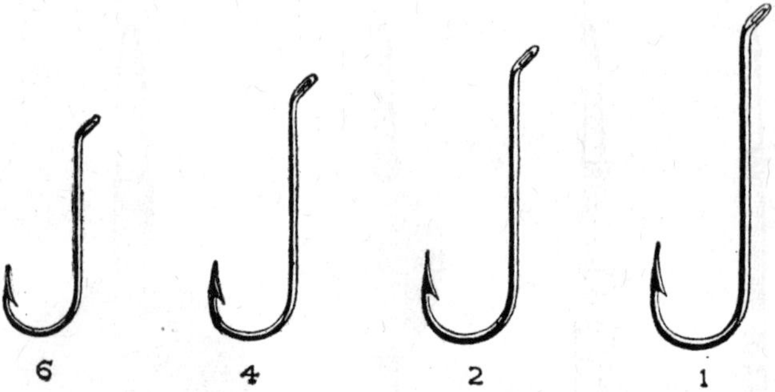

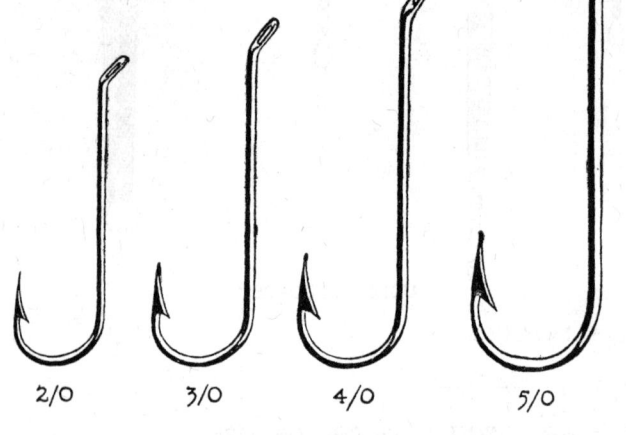

ROUND BEND HOOKS

Weights are as varied as all the other impedimenta of the angler; but a good start can be made with a box of assorted split shot, a few pierced bullets in various sizes, and a strip of ribbon lead wire. The last is sold in lengths a little over an inch wide from which one tears off pieces as required; these pieces are wound round the trace or line and for some purposes are superior to split shot. Split shot, unless very carefully closed, are always liable to damage the cast, and have a further disadvantage in that they are sometimes mistaken for food by the fish, particularly when using such baits as hemp or elderberries.

A landing net should be the next article purchased and, in choosing one, see that it has a wide opening, a deep pocket and a long handle. A wide opening is very important. To have hooked, say, an eight-pound pike whilst perch fishing and then to find that it is impossible to get it into the net by reason of its length is infuriating. A deep pocket is equally important if you wish to avoid seeing a large fish jump out again after you have got it into the net. The majority of landing net handles seem to have been made under the impression that the user will always be fishing either from a boat, or from a perfectly clear bank with no weeds between him and his fish; but it is possible to get them in two joints with a total length of up to eight feet when in use. A net with such a handle can be made to serve either for boat or bank fishing, one joint only being used in the former circumstance. I prefer a circular ring, though the triangular shape may be more convenient for travelling. Both can be obtained in collapsible form and it is advisable to use this type if one has to travel any distance to one's fishing. A minnow mesh at the bottom of the net is useful for obtaining live bait; but I have not yet met with one of this type which is really deep enough for big fish—thirty inches in depth is not too much if one is likely to meet with really large fish. On no account should one be satisfied with the folding, short-handled type of net favoured by trout anglers on the plea that it is easy to carry. These nets are excellent for their purpose and the circumstances under which they are generally used, which is for trout and whilst wading; but it is only on very rare occasions that one has to wade whilst coarse fishing and the net itself is rarely carried whilst one is actually fishing.

A net sling is useful only when one is roving; but in most cases the coarse fish angler remains in one spot for some length of time and his net is then placed on the bank close beside him ready for immediate use when required.

In many types of coarse fishing it is an advantage to put down the rod whilst waiting for a bite. Rod rests can be purchased for this purpose. They are certainly useful when the banks are muddy or when there is much damp herbage about to soak the reel and handle of the rod; but, on the whole, I prefer a short-forked stick pushed into the bank; it doesn't matter much if you do forget it when you are packing up in the dusk.

A winder is very useful for carrying ready-made-up sets of tackle. I prefer one with a box in the centre for holding shot, float-caps, etc.; these usually have divisions for four lines or sets of tackle. They have polished bone ends, so that the gut is not chafed, and metal bars, well within the edges, so that the hooks do not catch in other articles of one's equipment.

Hooks and gut lengths should be kept in some sort of pocket case, of which there are plenty of different styles to choose from. My own is hand-made, because I could not buy exactly what I wanted, and consists of a stout linen cover with parchment pockets. I made it sufficiently large to take my line winder and furnished it with strong tapes, so that I had all my hooks, casts, floats (except the very fat ones), and sinkers in one container. If one has too many separate articles to remember when packing up one's equipment, there is always the chance that some important item may be forgotten.

A plummet is almost essential if one is fishing in water of unknown depth. This article consists of a small block of lead furnished with a metal loop at one end and with a small piece of cork let into the other. It is used for ascertaining the depth of the swim and the method is to slip the hook through the metal loop and press the point of it into the cork. By lowering the tackle into the water with the plummet attached one can shift the float up or down, as the circumstances require, and so be sure that one is fishing at the exact depth desired. By bumping the plummet lightly on the bed of the stream one can also tell if the bottom is firm or muddy, which knowledge may make a considerable difference to one's success.

COARSE FISHING

LINE WINDER WITH CENTRAL BOX FOR FLOAT CAP, SPLIT-SHOT, ETC

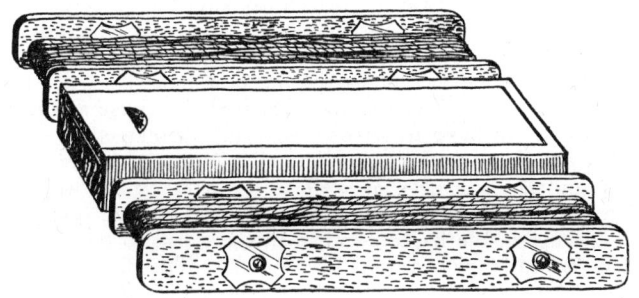

LEAD PLUMMET

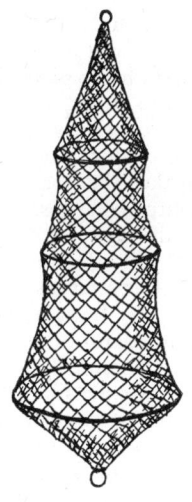

KEEP NET

If the fish caught are not required as food, they should be returned alive to the water, and a keep-net comes in useful here; in it the fish can be placed as caught and, at the end of the day, any required as specimens or food may be removed and killed and the remainder allowed their freedom.

For comfort and convenience the best type of carrier for tackle, bait and fish is a wicker-seat basket. These are very strong, comfortable to sit on and can be obtained in sizes sufficiently large to accommodate all equipment (other than rods and landing net), as well as one's lunch and a light waterproof. A detachable waterproof bag can be obtained for placing in the basket, and in this any fish to be used as food should be placed, thus keeping the inside of the basket clean. A satisfactory bag for this purpose can be made from an old mackintosh. Failing a bag, either bought or home-made, a cloth serves very well on which to wipe one's hands and in which to wrap the fish one wishes to take home.

For hook-baits and ground-baits of a vegetable nature, I use the small linen bags in which breakfast cereals are, or used to be, sold; but suitable small bags can be made at home from odd pieces of old linen. Worms and insect baits I carry in small tins with holes pierced in the lids.

With regard to floats, particularly quill floats, those displayed in the tackle shops usually have bright red tips. Red is an attractive colour and no doubt has a selling value; it also usually makes the float quite visible to the angler, but not under all circumstances. I have found that it is an advantage to paint the extreme tip of the float black and add a broad, bright yellow band below. The combination of yellow and black is a favourite " warning " colour scheme in nature, and we may be sure it is therefore most conspicuous under almost all conditions.

The modern " antenna " floats, which consist of a celluloid body with a thin extensible " antenna " on top, are a considerable improvement on the simple quill and particularly handy for use in windy weather. By removing the stopper at the top of the body of the float and half-filling the cavity with water, or shot, the float is steadied and the cast should be weighted so that the float swims just under the surface of the stream. The antenna is then extended and serves as an indicator of the bite. But these floats, or all that I have seen up to the present, have one slight defect. Since the line comes off from the top of the float, it follows that a part of it, at any rate, even if it has been well greased, will be below the surface of the water because the top of the float itself is under water. This length of drowned line will set up a drag and cause a delayed action in the strike. To get over this difficulty a thin wire loop should be whipped on just below the top of the antenna and the line passed through this; or a small rubber ring made from a piece of tubing will serve almost as well. The portion of line immediately next to the float will now be clear of the water and will in no way hinder the speed of the strike.

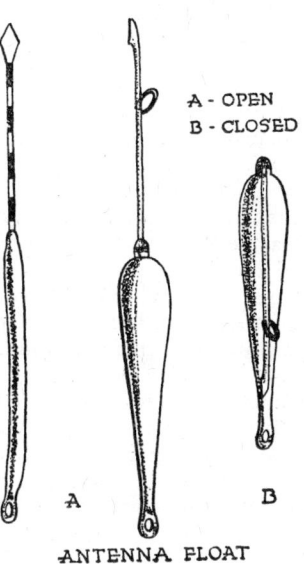

A - OPEN
B - CLOSED

ANTENNA FLOAT

"Mucilin" is a very good preparation for making the line float; and it is essential that the line *should* float, since it is quite impossible to strike quickly with even an inch or two of line beneath the surface. Some people use vaseline, but this is rather messy. For those who like making their own tackle and aids to angling, a good mixture is a piece of melted wax candle thoroughly mixed with vaseline until it is about the consistency of lard or margarine. A small piece of cloth kept in the tin and rubbed lightly up and down the line a few times before commencing fishing will render the line waterproof. Mutton kidney fat is also good and will be found much easier to apply if a little vaseline is worked in with it. I have found a piece of actors' cocoa-butter quite effective. Should the line sink after some hours' use, perhaps because of rain or the wind washing wavelets over it, it pays to stop fishing for a few moments, dry off the line carefully, either by wiping it in a dry cloth or holding it into the wind for a minute or two, and then giving it another coat of dressing.

Another useful addition to the coarse fish angler's equipment is a fairly stiff, but light, trout fly-rod. It should be eight or ten feet in length and should have a reel and dressed silk line to match. The line may be either tapered or level; it depends largely on how much money you are prepared to spend. The tapered line is, of course, the better article; but this does not mean that you cannot do good work with an untapered, or level, line. Some of the most successful anglers I have ever met have never possessed a tapered line. This fly-rod and its equipment will often turn an otherwise blank day into a successful one. It frequently happens that, though the fish are not feeding on the bottom and refuse to be tempted by your baits, there are rudd, dace and chub, and sometimes even roach and perch, ready to take a fly of the right type suitably presented. The trout rod may also be used for light float-fishing under circumstances, such as beneath trees or close under banks, where a longer rod would be a nuisance.

In what I have already written I have scarcely mentioned the pike, the "big game" fish of the coarse fish angler in the British Isles. The reason for this is that very little of the tackle so far mentioned is suitable for pike fishing. I propose dealing with this in a separate section on pike fishing.

Chapter III

WHERE TO FISH

A KNOWLEDGE of where fish are likely to be found is invaluable to the angler, no matter what type of fish he aims to catch.

As a broad principle the two most important factors are a clean hard bottom and a nice flow of water. As a matter of fact the two usually go together. But, even with a good flow of water, a cold clayey bottom is not usually favoured by fish of any sort. Weeds also prove an attraction; but they must be the right sort of weeds and limited in quantity.

In this connection weir pools at once spring to mind. They invariably have clean hard bottoms, a good flow of well-aerated water, deeps for retirement and, at the tail, clean shelving shallows on which the fish may bask and feed in the sun. Such weeds as may grow in weir pools do so around the edges, providing hiding places for pike and feeding ground for many species of water insects on which fish feed. There are also often trees overhanging the pool from which land insects, caterpillars, wood-lice, earwigs, etc., fall into the water. The wash of the water in weir pools usually renders necessary a few piles in places to protect the banks. Thick water-moss grows on the piles and on the stonework of the weir itself and freshwater shrimps congregate in the moss. Is it to be wondered that weir pools often provide some of the best fishing in a river?

But, of course, weir pools are not the only places in which to find fish. There are also runs between weed beds, corners where the current is turned away from the bank, shelters under overhanging trees, along the edges of bullrush beds, where ditches and field drains empty into the main stream: in all such places fish are likely to be found.

Sometimes, in long and fairly deep stretches full of weeds, openings may be found into which fish of many sorts come to feed from time to time. If one is a stranger to the water it is often a good plan to give all such places a short trial in the hope of hitting upon a favoured opening.

Just outside the little bays dug in the banks to enable cattle to drink is often a profitable spot to fish, particularly just after the cattle have been there.

When the river is full the fish keep out of the current and may then be found in the stiller parts and eddies. If the water is just over the bank in places and rather muddy fine fish may often be taken feeding over the submerged grass, though the water at the spot may be little over a foot deep. Under such conditions I have even taken them in a flooded road !

Small eddies frequently form pitching places for all sorts of submerged objects, including drowned insects and other foods. If one examines such a spot when the water is clear one can sometimes see a little heap of silt collected at the spot, just as sediment will settle in a heap in a tumbler of water if an eddy is formed by stirring. Fish in the neighbourhood know of these places and come to them from time to time in order to pick up anything edible which may have been deposited.

The entrances to pools are always the favourite feeding places of the fish inhabiting them; but, if the pool is very large, it often takes some time to draw the fish to this spot. This drawing is done by throwing in from time to time small quantities of food similar to that on the hook, but in not quite such an attractive form.

In ponds, the edges of water-lily beds, the vicinity of belts of rushes, and near where trees overhang are good spots to try.

Canals often present such a featureless appearance that it seems to be just a matter of luck if one happens to hit upon a spot occupied for the moment by fish. But, as a matter of fact, there are favoured spots even in canals. If one has not the assistance of a local angler, one can only discover these spots by trial; but, once such a spot is discovered, it is as well to mark it carefully by getting two conspicuous objects in the surrounding country into line, one on either bank, or by noting the position of some particular plant by the waterside, fence in the surrounding fields, or some other fixed and easily recognisable object.

The depth of the water must be considered with reference to the time of the year. During warm weather, even during the warmer part of a winter's day, fish frequently move into very much shallower water than when the water is cold.

There is an exception to the general rule that fish prefer to feed on a clean gravel bottom. This is the case of carp, tench and eels. All these fish may be taken over mud and frequently seem to prefer this type of bottom to any other. This must not be taken to mean that other fish may not be taken at times over mud. But, given the choice, you will be more likely to find fish over the one than over the other.

The arches of bridges and the pools below are generally good spots; but the fish frequenting them may not be at all easy to catch. These places form such convenient fishing spots that they are usually well attended by anglers and the fish around them soon become well educated.

A very strong current rarely holds fish for long. They may come there to feed from time to time; but they retire again to the calmer water to rest as soon as they have satisfied their hunger.

Boats, though sometimes alarming to fish when passing by, are often an attraction to them when moored in one spot for a sufficient length of time to allow the fish to become accustomed to them. Fish seem to approve of the shade afforded by a boat, and a punt moored throughout the summer at one place usually forms a shelter for some of the fish in the vicinity.

Cattle standing in the shallows often attract fish and, if there is a pool immediately below the shallows, the fish in it may be expected to come on the feed soon after the cows are seen to enter the water.

Places where people frequently bathe are often excellent in which to fish and a visit immediately after the swimmers have left the water is usually productive of sport.

In pools, the direction and force of the current flowing in at the head should be carefully studied. If the flow-in is of only moderate force, fish may be expected to come to feed right in it; but, if it is swift for the type of river, even if it appears to be swift only in the top layers of water, the fish are more likely to feed just at the edge of the current where particles of food are swept aside and begin to settle.

As the weeds begin to decay in the first frosts of winter, fish tend to move away from their vicinity and may be found in such parts of the water as are always devoid of weeds, or from which the weeds have already been swept.

It is, of course, impossible to lay down rigid rules as to where fish may, or may not, be found. Each stream, pond, river or canal has its own peculiarities. But in most cases the fish will be present or absent mainly in accordance with the brief outline of conditions I have given.

Chapter IV

COARSE FISHING

FLOAT-FISHING

THE most popular and most generally successful method of taking coarse fish is by float-fishing. At its simplest it consists of merely putting a worm on a hook suspended a foot or two beneath a cork float, putting the rod in a forked stick and sitting back to await results. Splendid fish are often taken by this method; but it can hardly be called fishing, though it may rightly be called catching fish. At the other extreme is an art of such a high degree of skill that only years of practice and attention to the smallest details can bring it to perfection.

All species of coarse fish can be taken by float-fishing, though the actual proceedings may vary considerably according to the nature of the fish desired and the place in which it lives. In still, or almost still water, and when using a worm as bait, the hook should be as near the bottom of the water as possible. Fish may occasionally be taken with the worm suspended somewhere about mid-water; but this is obviously most unnatural and such few fish as are caught are usually quite small. In order to get amongst the larger specimens it is advisable to ascertain the correct depth with the plummet and then to adjust the tackle so that the worm drifts along just clear of the bed of the stream, or hangs suspended within a fraction of an inch of the bed of the pond or canal. But, where the stream is fairly rapid the worm may be well off the bottom, for in such places worms and other food are swept along at a speed which prevents them from sinking other than very slowly. Perch sometimes prove an exception to this and, when really hungry, will take a worm in perfectly still water suspended several feet from the bottom.

If perch are the quarry the float may be either the simple egg-float, or the egg-float with a porcupine-quill centre. The hook should be *fairly* large if worm is to be the bait, sizes

2 to 6, according to the size of the worm. Perch have large but tender mouths, and if the hooks are too small the fish will quickly shake free. Perch travel in shoals and most of the fish in a shoal are nearly the same size. One of them seems to be the recognised leader and this is usually the one which is the first to bite. If this fish breaks free, it almost always departs and takes the rest of the shoal with it. The cast need not be finer than 2X or 3X; if perch intend to bite they are rarely put off by the sight of the cast attached to the bait and, as it is always advisable to get the hooked fish away from the shoal as quickly as possible, something fairly strong is needed to enable one to put on the pressure with safety directly the fish is hooked. The cast should be shotted about eight inches from the bait so that the float stands upright in the water, ribbon lead wire may be used in place of shot. The bite of a perch is usually indicated by a quick bob of the float, then a pause, then another two quick bobs followed by another pause, and finally a steady movement downwards and away. On no account should the line be checked in any way until the float moves off in the third phase of the bite and then the strike should be made as the fish is travelling, so as to ensure that the hook comes back towards the angle of the jaw where it is more likely to hold.

If a minnow, or other small fish, is used as a bait when float-fishing for perch it should be hooked through both lips. The same procedure should be followed when the perch bites as when fishing with worm. A live minnow will often take perch which are seen resting at mid-water, where a worm suspended unnaturally high above the bottom will frequently alarm and cause them to depart from the spot. Two small minnows on one hook are sometimes better than one large one.

Where perch are seen feeding around piles, or against a moss-covered wall, they may sometimes be taken by using a freshwater shrimp as bait. In this case a hook size 6 is about right, though a smaller size may be used if the bait is small. The shrimp should be hooked through the tail and the perch struck directly the float disappears.

In weir pools, around bridges, near old walls and where there are piles driven in to support the banks, are all good places in which to fish with the freshwater shrimp, and a wide variety of fish may be taken with this bait. To obtain a supply of shrimps, the best plan is to rake out a lump of watercress—if there are shrimps living in the water they are almost sure to be found in the clumps of watercress by the shallows, or in the ditches flowing into the main stream.

A wide variety of land insects form excellent baits for coarse fish. At the head of the list I should put blue-bottle flies and their near relatives, small green caterpillars, earwigs and the softer type of wood-lice. All these insect baits can be used when float-fishing and can be fished at almost any depth.

A practice I have sometimes followed when fishing in a strange river is to catch up a few insects and then to start roving along the banks, dropping in at the likely looking spots. In this way I can often discover where the roach are, or a good dace swim, or the haunt of some big chub.

The large flies and caterpillars are for summer fishing, as it is only in the summer that they are easily come by; but earwigs and wood-lice are excellent winter baits. The flies may be caught in a small net made from a piece of butter-muslin—a thing no bigger than a schoolboy's cap is quite sufficient; and the earwigs and wood-lice can be found beneath the bark of old fencing posts or fallen limbs of trees. The insects may be killed by giving them a nip on their heads and are as good dead as alive.

Having found the whereabouts of a shoal of roach by the method of floating an insect down the swim, I then try to discover if the fish are of a good size by plumbing the depth and letting the bait travel within two inches of the bottom. In almost every case the first fish taken has been a small one; but I shall probably soon know if there are better fish deeper down.

Float-fishing for roach can be a highly skilled performance; but this stage is not reached without a great deal of attention to detail and considerable practice. There are several styles favoured in different parts of the country. What is known as the Nottingham style is by fishing "fine and far off". A light rod is used and the tackle is both light and fine. Since the swim to be fished by this method is usually well out into the stream, the depth cannot be discovered by the use of the plummet. The method to be adopted is to estimate the depth and put the float rather higher than you think will be necessary. The tackle is then cast out and allowed to drift down the swim. If the float cocks at once, you know that at any rate your weights are off the bottom, otherwise the float would lie flat on the surface. But, if the bait is dragging, the float will duck a time or two and then draw under. If the distance between your lowest shot and the hook is eight inches, you should now lower the float four inches and try again. If it still bobs a time or two and finally draws under, lower the float a further two inches. If it now travels down the swim without check, you will know that your bait is within about two inches of the bottom, which is just about where it should be.

In what is sometimes referred to as " tight lining ", a style of fishing followed on the Lea and some other rivers, no reel is used and the line is fastened to the top ring of a rod twenty feet long. In this case the top of the rod is always kept directly above the float and no part of the line is allowed to rest on the water. When a fish has to be landed, the bottom joint of the rod is, and sometimes the last two joints are, removed so as to enable the angler to reach the fish with his net ; the fish being brought to the net, of course, and not the net to the fish.

Provided the depth of the water, together with the distance between the float and the top of the rod is not greater, or only very slightly greater, than the length of the rod, a good idea for keeping the line tight and preventing any loops forming between the rings is to fasten a piece of matchstick to the line beyond the top ring, and then reel in the line until the matchstick is stopped by the ring. This greatly aids quick striking.

The bite of a large roach differs greatly from the bold bite of a perch, or even a chub. If the chub or the perch intend biting they usually do so without hesitation and the float goes down properly ; but a roach is quite capable of feeling the bait carefully with its lips and, if it notices any resistance, blowing it out again at once. The bite, therefore, is often only shown by a checking of the float and the strike must be instantaneous if a connection is to be made before the bait is blown out. In slow, running water a big roach will often pick up the bait and hold it before attempting to swallow it. In this case the float falls over gently on its side and an equally quick strike is necessary before the roach has had time to notice the weight of the shot.

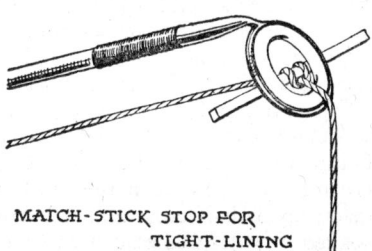

MATCH-STICK STOP FOR TIGHT-LINING

There is an enormous range of baits used for roach. Probably a great many new varieties are not yet discovered. Favourites amongst those of an animal nature are maggots, wasp grubs, small red worms and the tails of lobworms; these are all good winter baits and the red worms and tails of lobs may also be used when the water is coloured. Baits of a vegetable nature are more likely to succeed in summer and autumn. Amongst these may be mentioned bread-paste, creed-wheat, hempseed, elderberries and bread-crust, the last being also a very good winter bait. There are a great many others; but I think these may be considered the most generally favoured.

A certain amount of preparation is required before any of the above baits can be used. Worms should be scoured for a few days in damp moss; maggots should be cleaned in either bran or sand; wasp grubs should be gently steamed or baked until they are tough enough to be put on the hook without coming to pieces. Bread-paste should be made up at the water-side; it should be made from day-old bread and should be mixed with a little water from the river in a piece of clean rag; only the crumb of the bread should be used. Some anglers believe in coloured pastes, using cochineal or saffron as the colouring agent. A little of either goes a long way. I have done well with both; but it is almost impossible to say if success could justly be attributed to the colouring. Creed-wheat is best prepared by putting a teacupful of wheat into a thermos flask overnight and pouring boiling water on it; by morning the water will have been absorbed by the wheat and the grains will be in perfect condition for use on the hook. Hempseed can be prepared in the same way as wheat. Elderberries should be picked when ripe, kept on their stems and placed in a wide-mouthed preserving jar, adding a mixture of one part formalin and ten parts water. In baiting the hook with either creed-wheat or hempseed, care should be taken to see that the point of the hook penetrates the white seam and is slightly exposed, otherwise fish will be missed by failure to penetrate the tougher skin of the grain. Bread-crust is prepared from the bottom of a stale loaf. A slice made up of half crust and half crumb is cut from the loaf, soaked in water and placed under a flat weight for an hour or two; it is then cut into small cubes rather less than a quarter of an inch square. When baiting, the hook should be passed first through the crust and out through the crumb. In the preparing of roach-baits great care should be taken to see that everything is clean and free from taints, particularly that of tobacco.

Ground-bait is an essential feature of successful roach fishing and should consist of the same substance as the hook-bait, but coarser. Care should be taken to see that the ground-bait reaches the bottom at the same spot as the hook-bait. It should, therefore, be thrown in above where one is fishing. A much safer plan, however, is to squeeze a small lump of ground-bait, about the size of a fowl's egg, around the shot on the cast and lower it into the swim with the hook-bait; a gentle jerk will free the ground-bait and it and the hook-bait will then travel down the swim together. When fishing with either paste or crust a good ground-bait can be made in the nature of a cloud by drying some stale (but not sour) bread in a slow oven, crushing it into a fine powder and mixing with it some finely crushed egg-shells. This mixture is attractive to the fish, but has very little feeding value and therefore encourages them to take the more appetising hook-bait of a similar nature. Care should be taken to see that the ground-baiting is not overdone, otherwise the water may be fouled and the fish driven from the spot. Good results can often be obtained by baiting-up a swim a few days before one intends fishing it and at the same hour each day as that on which one will fish. With maggots and similar baits a few thrown in from time to time will keep the fish on the feed; but always try to avoid filling them up so that they cease biting because they are no longer hungry.

Dace may be caught on similar baits to roach; but they are usually found in swifter and shallower water. Though they keep in large shoals and many may frequently be taken in one place, they are, in my opinion, much more difficult to hook than roach. The bite is usually much more decided, the float disappearing with a quick bob, but the bait is equally quickly discarded, and again and again the angler finds that he is striking after the bait has been released by the fish. An angler who can hook one dace out of six bites may consider that he is doing quite well. Dace do not feed so closely to the bottom as do roach, and it is a good plan when fishing for them to change the depth at which the bait swims from time to time.

Bleak sometimes prove a nuisance to the float-fisher; but can usually be avoided by fishing close to the bottom. If they still persist in attacking the bait as it sinks, it may be necessary to change to a heavier float carrying a heavier weight. The heavier weight will carry the bait to the bottom before the bleak have time to take it.

SLIDER FLOAT

Gudgeon can be taken readily on float-tackle, the bait being a small, red worm, or maggot, fished right on the bottom. By raking the gravel and stirring it up the fish may be collected and brought on the feed. Though gudgeon are too small to put up a fight, they are one of the best of all freshwater fish as food, if properly cooked. They are also of great value as bait for both perch and pike.

Carp, bream, barbel and chub may also be taken on float tackle; but, as some form of ledgering, or float-ledgering is the method usually employed, I will deal with them separately under that heading.

For fishing in very deep water a sliding

float has to be used. This float, instead of being fixed by a cap to one point on the line, has two wire loops, one at the bottom and the other about three-quarters of the way towards the top, through which the line slides. The float is stopped at the required point by means of a small piece of rubber band, or a bristle, which is attached to the line and which is small enough to pass through the rings of the rod but too large to pass through the loops on the float.

Methods

LEGERING AND FLOAT-LEGERING

LEGERING is a method of angling in which the bait is anchored to one spot in the stream, instead of being allowed to drift along with the current as in float-fishing. If a float is used in this style of fishing it is called float-legering. In some cases it is not a method productive of great numbers of fish; but it is often very much better for securing the really large specimens. The rod is generally put down or placed in a rod-rest for this type of fishing, and it is, therefore, sometimes a welcome change from the somewhat stern concentration required in fishing with a moving float.

The tackle consists of a hook at the end of the cast and a pierced bullet, or flat ledger lead (the word appears to be spelt either with, or without the " d "; originally it was spelt without the " d " and, if it is derived from the Latin *legere*, as has been claimed, this would appear to be more correct; even if it is derived from the dialect word " leggen " or " liggen ", meaning " to lie down ", the old style appears equally correct) placed on the cast a foot to three feet above the hook. The bullet or ledger lead is kept in position by means of a shot pinched on below it. Some of the modern pierced bullets have a very wide bore, enabling the cast to move freely through when a fish takes the bait. When using these wide-bored bullets a small piece of matchstick should be looped to the cast below the weight to keep it in place.

It is an advantage, particularly when perch are about, to attach another hook some distance above the weight on which is placed a live minnow or gudgeon. The tackle may now be spoken of as a ledger-paternoster.

COARSE FISHING

Ledger-tackle is chiefly used for fishing in still water, in deep pools, or when it is necessary to fish a long distance from the bank. But if the spot chosen has a rather strong stream, it is always best to use the flat ledger-weight in preference to the pierced bullet, as the latter may be rolled along the bottom. It may also be necessary under such

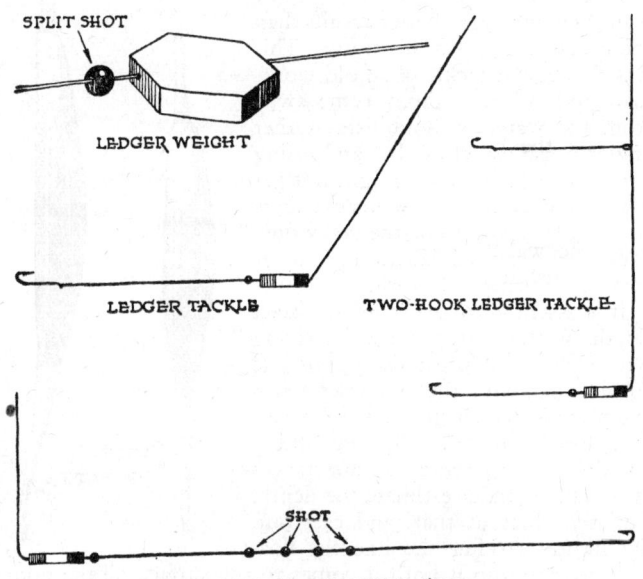

conditions to nip a few shot on to the cast near to the bait; but this should be only just sufficient to keep it from rising too high in the water.

The floats used for ledgering are usually fairly large and the tackle relatively heavy. This is quite right when one is expecting heavy carp or tench; but small floats and quite light tackle can be used for roach or rudd. It is largely a matter of using the type of tackle that fits in best with the conditions. Obviously it is foolishness to use very light tackle when fishing for tench close to weed beds into which they will certainly dash directly they are hooked; you must then have tackle on which you can put sufficient pressure to turn the fish, otherwise you will certainly be broken.

The mention of tench reminds me that it sometimes happens that a length of carpet-thread, or strong, fine line, between the hook and the cast, or main line, may give better results than the usual gut, or gut substitute. This was the regular tackle of an old workman and he very rarely came away from the water without fish. Other anglers fishing close by and using very much finer tackle might not get a bite; but even on the worst evenings he seemed always to be the lucky one. I can offer no explanation; but it certainly seemed to work.

It is essential to ascertain the exact depth of the water when ledgering with a float. It is not always possible to do this with the plummet when the place in which the bait is to rest is a long way off. The only thing to do under these circumstances is to rather under-estimate the depth, put the float at that, and cast out. By lightly jerking the line the float will now run up it until it comes to the surface. Take note now of the distance between the float and the top of the rod when the line is straight and recover the tackle without reeling in the line. It may be necessary to draw in the line by hand; but this length can be drawn back again through the rings when the tackle is on the bank. If the piece of rubber-band is now attached to the line at the same distance from the rod top as the float was when it rose to the surface, the line will be straight between the float and the weight when the tackle is again cast out, and any bites will be registered at once.

When summer ledgering for roach I usually bait with a

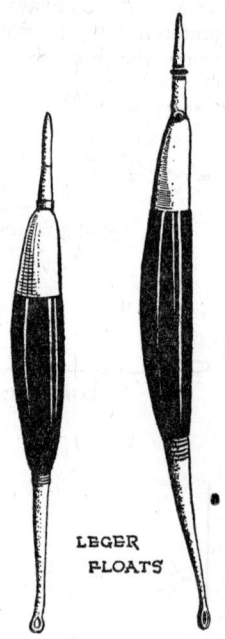

LEGER FLOATS

fair-sized piece of paste, particularly if I think there are many eels in the water; but in winter, or even in late autumn, I prefer to use a worm or the tail of a lob as I know that I am unlikely to be worried by eels at that time of the year. If I am ledgering for either perch or tench in summer (and it is not much use fishing for tench at any other time of the year), I always use a worm as bait. For perch I like a worm of only moderate size—say, about four inches in length; but for tench I like a really large lobworm. A larger hook is necessary when using a larger worm. Float-ledgering is usually the most satisfactory way of fishing for tench; they prefer to stay in almost still water, even in a river, and are so shy that it is advisable to allow the bait to remain in one place for a considerable time, rather than to keep moving it. The bite of a tench often starts with a few waving movements of the float, then the float sinks steadily and moves away. As the float moves off is the time to strike and not before. Sometimes the float continues to wave about for a long time without sinking and going off. It is useless to strike at this waving movement in the hopes of hooking the fish. My own belief is that when the float continues this waving and wobbling over a long period the tench are merely brushing the line with their bodies as they root about around the bait and that they do not have the bait in their mouths at all. Bubbles can generally be seen rising round the float at these times, indicating that the fish are feeding at the spot, though probably only on minute organisms in the mud.

The carp is another fish, very similar in habits to the tench, which may be taken float-ledgering. But the carp is even shyer than the tench and is rarely caught unless the angler takes most careful precautions against the fish discovering his presence. The bait may be a worm; but a far better bait is a parboiled young potato. Many expert carp anglers do not use a float; or, if they do, use only a small slice of bottle-cork, or some other small and natural-looking object. The depth must be accurately plumbed beforehand, as any disturbance of this nature is quite sufficient to drive the fish from the spot. Having thrown out the baited hook, the rod must be placed in a rod-rest and the angler is advised to sit back and prepare for a long wait. Even when the fish takes the bait it may be half an hour before it decides to swallow it and so give the angler the chance of hooking it. But there is very rarely any question when the fish has actually got the bait well into its mouth; the float goes down and the line rushes out at express speed. There is no need to strike, in fact there is a great danger of a break if one does so; all that is necessary is to take up the rod and check the line for an instant to drive home the hook. In order that there shall be no check to the line when the carp takes the bait, it is a good plan to pull a foot or two of line from the reel and let this lie loose on the ground; a small piece of paper placed across it will act as an indicator and, by its movement, show when the line is moving.

It is always advisable to bait-up the spot one intends fishing for several days beforehand when the quarry is either tench or carp, and the baiting should be done at the same time as one intends fishing; it is, in fact, almost useless to fish for carp without doing so. For tench, chopped worms are a good ground-bait, and for carp a mixture of bread and meal with a little of the hook-bait mixed in. The spot should be very carefully marked by anchoring a piece of rush upright in the middle, as it is useless baiting over an area more than a few yards either way.

In connection with both carp and tench, the lighter the weight used the better. If it is possible to cast accurately with no more than a couple of shot, that will be sufficient. The aim should be to cut down everything that may give the fish any idea that the bait is a trap of some sort. As a further aid to camouflage it is an advantage to see that the gut is as nearly the shade of the water as possible and the hook-length the same colour as the bottom, green or brown for weeds or mud respectively.

Early morning and late evening are the best times to fish for carp or tench and, of the two, early morning from daylight until the sun is up I consider the best.

The barbel is another fish which may be angled for by the ledger-method. Barbel are usually found in deep gravelly pools. Weir pools are especially favoured. They are very powerful fish and strong tackle is necessary as they fight extremely hard and always endeavour to get into weeds if there are any close by. But they are also very shy and it is therefore necessary to use as fine tackle as one dare (bearing in mind the possibility of hooking a fish of ten pounds, or even more). With these fish also it is necessary to ground-bait the swim for some days beforehand, worms being the usual bait. Some anglers have the swim baited-up for a week before they fish, vast quantities of worms being used in the process; but quite as good results may often be had by merely ground-baiting at the time of fishing. If possible the worms should not be thrown into the water, as barbel are easily alarmed. To ensure that the worms reach the right spot a good plan is to enclose a number in a cup of clay dug from the bank of the river, close the cup by pulling the edges of the clay together, and lower gently to the bottom by means of the weight on your ledger, pressing this into the clay and releasing it by giving it a slight jerk when the bottom is reached. If a boat is available, several closed clay cups of worms may be lowered into the swim before one commences fishing. The worms will find their way out gradually and so provide a steady supply of ground-bait. Where hempseed is regularly used by roach anglers a paste made with soaked bread and with a stewed hempseed pressed into it is often a very good bait. In the Thames, in the neighbourhood of house-boats, barbel are sometimes taken on a piece of fat bacon—or were before the 1 oz. per week days!

Bream are usually angled for by the float-ledgering method and the favourite bait is a good big lobworm. They feed chiefly at night and many keen bream fishers go out prepared to make a night of it. But they may also be taken during the daytime and particularly in the late evening. Bream run to a considerable weight, some having been taken weighing over ten pounds. It is therefore necessary to use strong tackle though they are not usually very fierce fighters. Immediately prior to feeding bream often come to the surface and sport. Many habitual bream anglers say that it is quite useless fishing for them unless they have first behaved in this manner.

The chub is another good subject for ledger-fishing, either with or without a float. Being the "fearfullest of fishes", it naturally follows that the method of angling most likely to meet with results with this fish is that which can be followed with least disturbance. The ledger fulfils this condition better than most others. Chub frequently inhabit relatively small and shallow pools amongst weeds. They will almost certainly retire beneath the weeds directly the angler approaches; but he may now put out his ledger-tackle, baited either with a lump of cheese paste, a good big worm, a cube of banana, stoned cherries in season, a live minnow or, in winter, the pith from the spinal-cord of a bullock. Sooner or later the chub will come out again from the shelter of the weeds, or perhaps the hollows under the bank, and, if the angler keeps well out of sight and his rod does not form a very conspicuous silhouette against the skyline, one of the shoal will almost certainly take the bait. If there are many chub pools in the vicinity, it often pays to move on to the next after having taken one fish as the disturbance of the one sometimes upsets the whole shoal for half an hour or more. But, if things can be so arranged that the fish is taken well outside the edge of the shoal or well below it, it is quite possible to capture several without alarming the rest.

Methods

PATERNOSTERING

The use of the paternoster is confined almost entirely to fishing for pike and perch.

The tackle consists of two or three hooks attached at intervals to a length of gut, or gimp, with a weight at the bottom. They can be obtained ready made, mounted on either gimp, or cable wire, and perhaps in gut, or gut substitute, as well; though I have not noticed this in the catalogues. I prefer to make up my own paternoster and am content with two hooks placed about a foot to eighteen inches apart. My method is to take a length of gut substitute of medium thickness and about four feet in length. I then make a loop at either end and two other loops at what I consider the best positions on the length; if the water is thick I tie the bottom loop quite close to the weight, so that the bait will lie right on the bed of the river; and if the water is clear I make it about eight or ten inches above the bait. The other loop is made about a foot to eighteen inches above the first, according to the depth of the water—the deeper the water the greater the distance between the two loops.

To the bottom loop I attach a pear-shaped lead weight, and to the other two loops I attach hooks, furnished with gut lengths, of a size suitable to the baits I am going to use. The line is attached to the top loop.

Since the lead weight is rather liable to get hung up in obstructions on the bottom an economy can be effected and

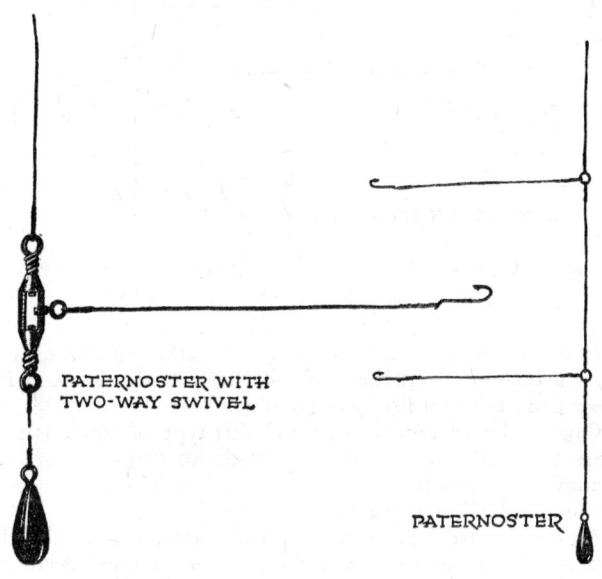

PATERNOSTER WITH TWO-WAY SWIVEL

PATERNOSTER

the rest of the tackle saved by using a small stone or an old iron nut attached to a piece of thin string or thread. Then, when the hang-up occurs the loss is only the stone or old nut. I get a good supply of nuts of all sizes on a hill I climb several times each week. The hill carries a lot of heavy motor traffic and it is surprising how many nuts get shaken off.

The usual baits are a worm on the bottom hook, and a minnow or small gudgeon on the top.

An excellent method of fishing with the paternoster is to drift quietly along in a boat over weeds and drop the tackle into the openings: or one can walk along the bank and fish the holes and corners.

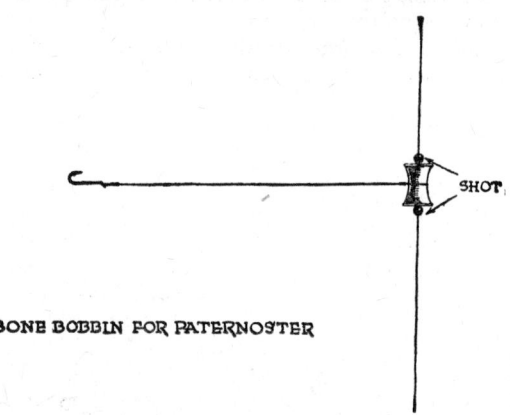

BONE BOBBIN FOR PATERNOSTER

It is advisable to use a long rod whether one is fishing from a boat or from the bank so that one can keep as far away from the spot fished as possible.

One of the advantages of using this type of tackle is that there is no necessity to plumb the depth and therefore no changing the position of the float each time one comes to deeper or shallower water.

The ready-made paternoster usually has the hook-lengths attached either to three-way swivels, or to bone beads or bobbins. There is certainly an advantage in the use of these when one is baiting with a live-bait, as the swivel or bobbin permits the bait to circle the main gut without getting wound around it. Both bobbins and swivels can be purchased separately and the tackle made up with either of them incorporated in it. But this means a good deal of extra knot-tying and, as I usually make up the tackle on the river bank when

COARSE FISHING

I come to a spot which appears suitable for its use, I prefer to do without them. I do, however, recommend their use when one is fishing fairly regularly by this method, and in this case, of course, the tackle should be assembled at home.

The attachment of the three-way swivels is by means of firm knots or whippings. The bobbins are pierced and they are threaded on to the gut and kept in place by split shot pinched on immediately above and below.

Some anglers use a float when fishing with a paternoster. The float is a small one and not sufficiently buoyant to raise the weight off the bottom. It must also be placed rather lower on the line than the depth of the water, but not so low as to render it invisible. I cannot see that there is much advantage, if any, by this use of a float. The "knock" of a biting fish can be felt quite distinctly through the rod and the float seems to me to be merely an additional encumbrance.

One must use judgment in timing one's strike when fishing for perch, and particularly so when using a paternoster. If you have any reason to believe that the fish are biting shyly, lower the point of the rod directly you feel a touch and do not attempt to strike until the fish moves off. And when you do strike, don't strike too hard. Perch have very soft mouths and it is very easy to pull the hook away from its hold. When this happens the fish takes fright and dashes away, and, in nearly every case, the other members of the shoal dash away after it and do not return.

For summer fishing with a paternoster it is almost essential to have a boat, for the fish are then usually to be found right out in the middle of the river amongst the weeds.

The most pleasant method is to get a companion to manage the boat and for him to guide it so that it drifts within reach of the openings in the weeds, though not over them. There will probably be a slight current—for perch do not care for absolutely dead water if they can find a little movement—and all that is necessary is to just steady the boat so that it hangs a little on approaching the selected spot. If a fish does not bite almost at once, move quietly on to the next likely opening and repeat the performance.

In places where the perch are very shy this drifting method is not of much use and one is up against the problem of how to keep the boat in one place for a considerable time without causing any disturbance, for one must exercise a great deal of patience with these fish. It is certainly not advisable to heave over a large weight to act as anchor; neither is it a good plan to thump the bottom with an iron-shod pole to make a stake to which the boat may be attached. I think the best method is to start lowering the anchor-weight overboard some little distance before the spot is reached and then to allow it to touch bottom gently in such a situation that the boat will pull up just the right distance from the place you wish to fish. A really skilful boatman is a great help under these conditions.

The paternoster sometimes comes in useful when fishing for chub in coloured water when the river is rather high. At such times the chub often get into the eddies. But in these places when the river is very full there is usually a very strong surface current which sweeps away a float or sucks it under in the swirls. By the use of a paternoster the bait can be anchored in the eddy where it can await the arrival of a fish cruising there in search of food.

Methods

FREE LINING

I HAD to invent a name for this because I have never heard it mentioned except by some description which would be much too long for use as a heading. Briefly, it consists of fishing without either a float or a weight, though it may be advisable to depart slightly at times from this rule by adding a few shot.

It is a method which is not very commonly used, partly, I suppose, because not many coarse fish anglers carry the necessary equipment with them, and also because it can be operated only under certain conditions which exist but very occasionally in coarse fish waters. But I think it might be used much more frequently than it is and I feel sure that those doing so will get a great deal of pleasure from it.

To begin with it is essential that you should have a rod with which you could cast a fly. It was because of this (and fly-fishing for coarse fish which will be referred to later) that I recommended the purchase of a trout fly-rod. Such a rod will not be an unnecessary luxury to the coarse fisher, for with it he can do light float-fishing as well as the method I propose describing and, of course, fly-fishing.

Free lining, as I have called it, consists of casting a bait just as one would a fly. The bait may be either grub, caterpillar, maggot, or worm; either of these may be regarded as more or less regular baits. The grubs may be either caddis, wasp grubs, or beetle grubs, the latter being found under dry cow pats. Under special circumstances freshwater shrimps, or even vegetable baits such as elderberries may prove successful.

The water must be relatively shallow and, for preference, should be in a sufficiently clear state to enable one to see what is happening, though a skilful angler can catch fish by merely watching the cast and tightening directly he sees it move off. Suitable spots are in the pits and runs between weed beds, under bushes and close to walls, bridges and moss-covered posts. Deep wide rivers are not suitable and usually only along the edges in ponds is it of much use to try this method. The hook, which should have the point fully exposed, should be of a size suited to the bait; that is to say, it must not be smothered by the grub, shrimp or worm. A tapered cast should be used and this should not exceed the length of the rod, though it is an advantage to have it considerably shorter than the rod if one is fishing a very small stream where one would probably have to get very close to the spot to be fished.

The approach should be made from downstream, moving slowly, keeping low, and taking advantage of even the smallest of cover, such as a thistle or dock plant. The bait should be cast into all the likely looking spots and allowed to drift down with the current. The fish will follow the bait down and, if it is not possible to actually see when it has taken the bait into its mouth, the line should be tightened directly it turns its head upstream again.

In casting one should remember that the heavier the bait the slower should be the action. Anything in the nature of a quick flip will either flick the bait from the hook or land it with a flop far short of the spot aimed at. It is as well to practise this on land before trying it on the fish. Hooks with barbed shanks are very useful for this style of fishing; but, if for any reason they cannot be obtained, a small piece of bristle or fine wire whipped to the top of the hook-shank will answer nearly as well.

In shallow water it may be possible to wade—it may even be advisable to wade if the river is so wide that very little of it can be covered from the bank. But as a general rule I think wading should be avoided when dealing with coarse fish. Most coarse fish, with the exception of pike, move about in shoals, and if you alarm one fish you probably alarm the whole shoal of them.

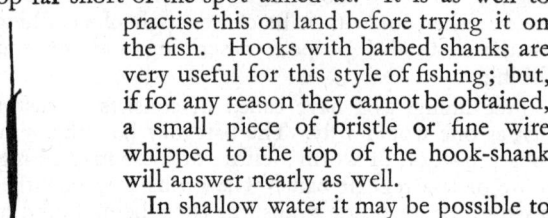

HOOK WITH BARBED SHANK

Chub, dace and perch are the most likely fish to be taken by this means. Chub must be most carefully approached and great care should be taken not to place the bait right in front of them. If one can cast accurately enough to let it fall about six inches or a foot on the near side of the fish, and about level with its shoulder, nine times out of ten it will be taken without hesitation.

If perch are seen slowly cruising near the surface under bushes they will usually take a worm or caterpillar presented by this method. They may also be taken with the freshwater shrimp near bridges and piles. In this case it is usually essential to add a few shot to the cast to make the bait sink to the required depth. As it will now be unlikely that the bait will be visible to the angler he must strike directly he sees a movement of the line suggesting that a fish has taken hold.

Under whatever circumstances this method is followed it is essential that direct contact with the bait should be maintained throughout by raising the rod top at a pace in keeping with the pace of the stream.

The best worms to use are either the small green marsh worms, generally found in damp clayey ground and almost always partly curled up, or the worm known in some parts as the "black head". This worm is also a dweller in clayey ground, often alongside roads in the damp spots close to the hedge, and has a cold-looking blue head; it is very tough and not readily damaged by casting, but it should not be used in its larger sizes. If small lobworms are used they should be well toughened in moss for some days beforehand. Brandlings I cannot recommend. They are much too delicate.

Under this heading may well be described a method which sometimes proves very successful with rudd.

Rudd are to be found usually close to overhanging bushes, or beside lily beds. They feed on or near the surface and are extremely shy: but fortunately they are generally ready biters provided the angler can keep out of sight. A boat is almost a necessity for this type of fishing and a companion on the bank often a great help. The helper on the bank should throw small pieces of dry bread on to the water above the haunt of the fish so that the bread drifts over the spot and brings the rudd on to the feed. The angler in the boat must now cast a hook baited with a piece of dry bread so that it travels down with the others. A piece with some crust attached will be more likely to remain on the hook than crumb alone. Long-distance casting is necessary and also considerable skill and patience: but it is a very interesting method and the fish themselves are usually good fighters.

If the rudd live in a lily bed a movement of the leaves may sometimes be noticed showing that the fish are swimming about beneath them close to the surface. When this happens, select an opening between the leaves somewhere close to where the fish are seen to be moving and cast your baited hook so that it rests on the leaf *beyond* the opening, with the cast resting on the leaves between you and the opening. Let the bait, which may be either a piece of bread or a maggot, remain for a few moments on the lily leaf, then quietly draw it so that it falls into the little gap between the leaves. A fish will presently come along and take the bait, when the cast will be seen to be drawn across the lily pads. The strike should not be violent as it is quite possible that the fish may be a fairly large carp. It is as well to select an opening close to the outer edge of the lily bed so as to be able to get the fish away from them into more open water as quickly as possible.

Methods

SPINNING

APART from pike, which will be dealt with later, perch are almost the only coarse fish which can be taken by spinning. At times chub will take a spinning bait, but in my experience

FISHING IN OPENING IN WATER-LILY BED

A — FIRST POSITION

B — BAIT MOVED TO FALL BETWEEN LEAVES

they do not do so with sufficient regularity to make it worth while spinning for them of set purpose. Though I have fished a good deal in water well stocked with large chub, I have only taken them occasionally by spinning when fishing for perch and sometimes when fishing for pike.

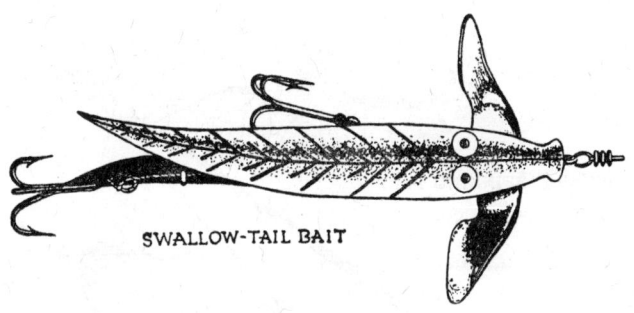

SWALLOW-TAIL BAIT

The favourite spinning baits for perch are metal Devon minnows, quill or silk phantoms, or small copper spoons about an inch and a half in length. They will take quite large pike spoons: but a large proportion of fish which come at these relatively large baits will not be hooked. Far better to

COLORADO SPOON

use the rather stiff fly-rod I have recommended and some form of spinning bait of such a size that it does not overpower the rod. A light metal Devon, not more than two inches in length, will be just about right for this work, or a two-inch phantom. A small "Swallow-tail" bait is also good for this type of fishing. I do not think there is much to be said for any particular colour; but I like to have at least two to choose from in case the fish show a preference.

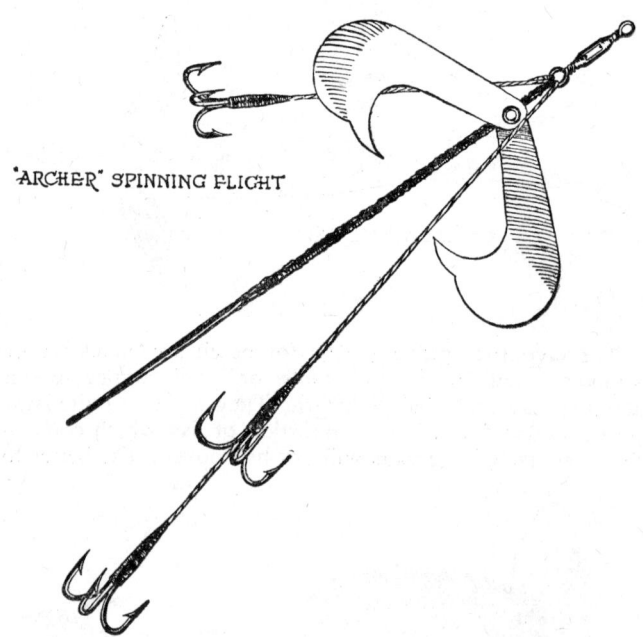

"ARCHER" SPINNING FLIGHT

If the perch are lying fairly close to the surface, as they often do during the summer months, the phantom or "Swallow-tail" is the best type of bait to use, because it sinks slowly and enters the water with very little disturbance. During the winter months, when the perch frequent deeper water, a Devon or weighted spoon must be used in order to get down to them. There are a good many varieties of spoons suitable for perch spinning. I prefer one of bright copper, or one with copper outside and silver inside. I do not like a weight outside the bait when spinning for these fish as the fish themselves will often run at the weight instead of the bait, and it is difficult to make such a quiet cast with the bait and weight separate.

The trace should not be finer than 1X drawn gut and should be fitted with at least three swivels, that is to say, a double swivel in the centre and an ordinary single swivel at the end to which the line is tied. If the spinner itself has not a swivelled attachment link, there should be another swivel at the other end of the trace to which the bait can be attached, a spring link swivel is the best for this.

The line should be plaited, of about six pounds breaking strain, and may be either dressed or undressed. The best reel is one of the multiplier type with a wide drum. With these reels one can cast quite light baits with ease.

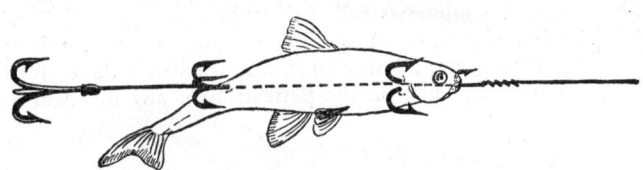

SPINNING FLIGHT WITH MOVABLE LIPHOOK

Preserved or natural minnows are also used fitted to flights of hooks of the "Archer" type, which consists of a spear with spinning fins attached and three triangles. With this type of spinning flight the drive for the spin comes from the head of the bait. A simpler, and in some ways better, type of flight consists of two or three triangles, one behind the other, and a movable lip hook. In this case the drive comes from the tail of the bait, which is curved round so as to offer resistance to the water and so causes the bait to revolve. The lip hook is moved up or down according to the size of the bait.

In order to prevent kinks in the line it is a good plan, if you make up your own traces, to put a half-circle of sheet celluloid on the trace just below one of the links. Two holes are drilled in the celluloid at either end of the straight edge and the gut passed through these; this will act as a keel and compel the swivels below it to keep in action so that no turns can be given to the line. If a ready-made trace is used a fold-over, or zig-zag lead may be fitted to the trace, again, just below a swivel, preferably the top one.

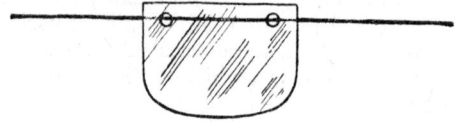

CELLULOID 'KEEL' FOR
ATTACHING TO SPINNING TRACE

If a spinning reel is not used, a method of dealing with the line, which is sometimes called the "Devon style", is soon learned and very interesting in operation. I prefer this to spinning from a reel because success in it entirely depends on my own skill and not on the perfection of any mechanism.

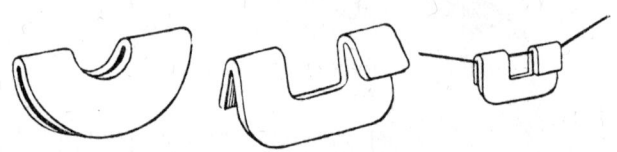

FOLD-OVER AND ZIG-ZAG LEAD WEIGHTS

To perform the operation a length of line is drawn from the reel and the bait cast out. The recovery is effected by taking the line between the first finger and thumb of the left hand, bringing forward the little finger until it engages the line a few inches farther forward, taking this point also between the finger and thumb, and reaching forward again with the little finger to take up another few inches. The recovered loops of line lie in the palm of the left hand and are drawn off again when the next cast is made. This may sound very complicated, but a few minutes' practice with a piece of string will soon prove that it is not really very hard to learn. It was the method employed by all the old native Devon anglers, none of whom had more than one reel and one line to serve all purposes, and the reel, of course, was one of the usual metal ones with fixed check with which it was impossible to cast any distance from the reel itself.

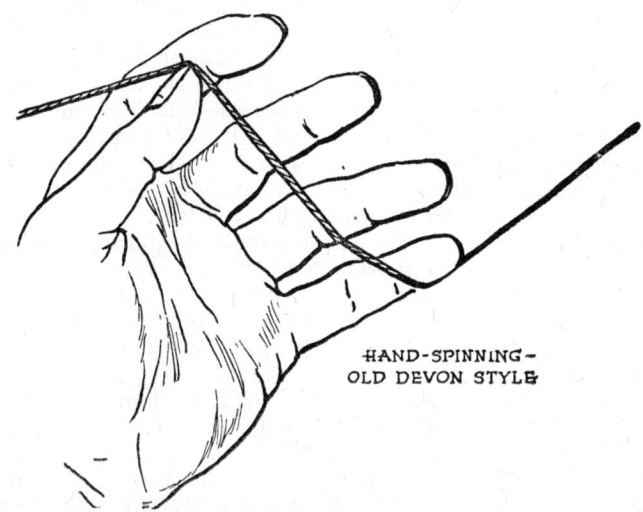

HAND-SPINNING—
OLD DEVON STYLE

The usual method of spinning for perch is to cast out the bait into the likely spot and recover it, not too quickly, so that it travels steadily through the area to be fished. A variant of this is the "sink and draw" method. In this style the bait is cast out and allowed to sink to the bottom. It is then recovered a distance of two or three feet by raising the rod top at the same time recovering two or three feet of line. It is then allowed to sink again and the lifting operation repeated until all the line has been recovered. The bait spins up from the bottom and sinks again as if it was a small fish either wounded or playing. A natural minnow is the best bait for this, a preserved one being the next best.

Perch may also be caught by the "thread-line" method of spinning, though I personally consider it unsuitable. I shall describe this more fully under "Pike".

Methods

FLY-FISHING

An increasing number of coarse fish anglers are discovering the pleasure to be obtained from the use of the artificial fly. Amongst the fish to be caught by this method are chub, dace, rudd, perch, roach, and even under certain conditions, pike.

The equipment required consists of the fairly stiff trout fly-rod I have already mentioned and this must be fitted with a metal or plastic reel of the best possible balance to suit the rod. The balance of the reel and rod is of much greater importance in fly-fishing than when a float is used. Any serious departure from this rule is soon felt by the angler in a quickly tiring arm and an inability to put his fly just where he wants it. The line must be a plaited and dressed one; but the question of whether it should be level or tapered largely depends on the financial position of the purchaser. The cast should be, for preference, tapered, and should be of a thickness suited to the fish one intends catching: for chub it should certainly not be finer than 3X and for perch the same; it is usually perfectly safe to use 4X for rudd, dace and roach.

The selection of flies need not be great. I pin my faith almost entirely on three, merely varying the size according to the circumstances. These three are the Coch-y-bondhu, Black Gnat and Alder. Greenwell's Glory is another excellent fly for use in fishing for coarse fish. With the exception of the Alder, all my flies are dressed with hackles only—no wings.

Starting with the chub, I rarely use anything but a large Coch-y-bondhu dressed on a No. 6 or No. 7 hook. The hackles should be nearly an inch in length and the fly, as with all the others, should be dressed fairly full so as to ensure perfect floating. I make my own flies and use stiff cock's hackles only, which ensure good floating capabilities.

The finest of all chub fishing is to be had in late September, or early October, the latter month for preference. By this time the chub will have fully recovered from their spawning and will be in the best possible condition. At about this time of the year also the daddy-long-legs are usually hatching and my long-hackled Coch-y-bondhu makes a very good imitation of one of these insects.

The method to follow is to walk quietly upstream, facing the sun if possible (or at any rate with the sun shining from the opposite bank), and to stalk the suitable spots with the greatest possible caution. It is impossible to take too much trouble in the approach; chub are extremely wary and

WHERE THE FLY SHOULD ALIGHT

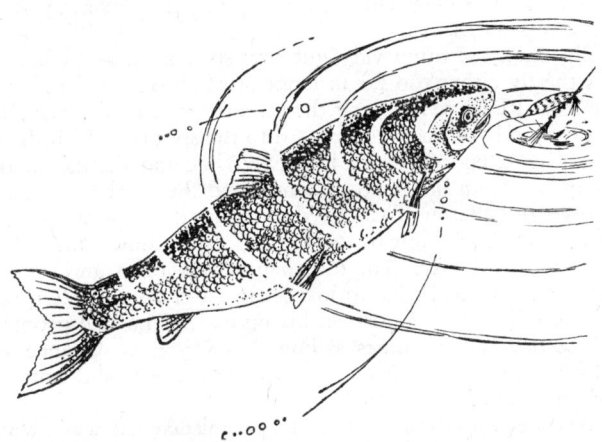

nervous fish and once they detect the presence of the angler it is useless for him to expect to get them to take what he is offering. On the other hand, if he moves with such care that the fish have no idea he is near, it really doesn't matter if the fly does fall with rather a flop. The nearest chub is almost sure to take it! The flags growing beside the water, the bushes on the banks and even the taller weeds in the meadows should all be made use of as cover for approach. The rod also must be kept as low as possible, using a side cast rather than the more usual overhead cast.

Mention of the nearest fish taking the fly suggests another important point. Do not fish blindly at a shoal of chub if you can by any means get a sight of them and note the exact position of the larger fish. Even then, do not fish straight away for them, naturally picking the biggest and hoping it will be the one to grab your fly. No, sit down quietly and watch the movement of the shoal. In almost every case it will be found that individual fish, often the largest, move off from the main body from time to time. When you have made pretty sure of their usual course, move quietly into such a position that will enable you to cast for one of these larger fish without disturbing the others. And when you have hooked him, for the same reason try to play him away from his companions.

Big chub are often very gut shy, so it is advisable not to put the fly either too far in front or at all on the far side of the fish. I believe in taking the utmost care that the cast shall be absolutely correct with regard to the spot on which the fly is to alight, and that spot is between me and the fish, about six inches from him, and rather behind the level of his head. It does not matter if the fly does come down with rather a bang; often so much the better, as it draws immediate attention to the fly. The fish then usually turns and grabs it before he has had time to inspect it. A chub will often take a fly which drops almost on his nose; but he will probably refuse one which comes sailing down from a distance and which gives him plenty of time to examine it and note the gut to which it is attached.

Another important point: do not mistake the wave which will often envelop the fly for the nose of the chub and strike directly you see the fly disappear. A large chub displaces a lot of water and his nose is usually preceded by a fairly large bulge. If you can actually see the fish, wait until it turns away before striking. But, if the fish itself is invisible, pause just a half-second before you tighten or you will be almost certain to draw the fly away from it.

Should the day be breezy, fish the edges of lily beds and any spots affording under-water cover. Always wait until the surface is ruffled by the wind, even if it means sitting down for ten minutes or longer. A long stretch of still water known to hold chub can often provide considerable sport if a day of light breezes is selected.

The technique of fly-fishing for dace differs considerably from that employed when chub is the quarry. The dace usually inhabits rather shallower water and rarely keeps close to any shade. Broad shallows, streamy bits between weed beds, eddies and the shallowing tails of pools are likely places. The dace also is a very quick riser and one must strike with the greatest speed if one is to effect its capture. My favourite fly for dace fishing is the black gnat, and it is an advantage to have this dressed on a small double hook, size 0 or 00. Even with this double hook the proportion of missed rises is remarkably high; but fortunately the dace will often rise again and again if not actually touched by the hook. If they refuse the black gnat but are seen to be still rising, a change should be made to a small Coch-y-bondhu, or small Greenwell's Glory. I must emphasise the word small, for the dace has a small mouth and it is therefore of no use to try to catch it with a large fly.

Fly-fishing for dace is one of the few methods of fishing for coarse fish in which it often pays to wade. This is particularly so when one is fishing the tail of a pool. But it is essential to remember that the fish are in a shoal and that therefore frightening one may mean frightening the lot.

Up to the present I have assumed that the angler is doing his fly-fishing from the bank, except when he may happen to be wading. But the use of a boat is almost an essential in fly-fishing for rudd. In narrow streams they can be tackled as they lie under their sheltering bushes by casting from the opposite bank; but in broader waters and ponds one must have a boat in order to get within reach of them. Rudd will take almost any small fly, but great care must be taken not to alarm them by an incautious approach or by rocking of the boat when fishing. Needless to say a punt is always to be preferred to a boat with a keel. Rudd will often rise very freely to the fly during the evening of a warm day. The size of the hook should not exceed No. 1.

Roach are not nearly such free-risers as either dace or rudd. Many anglers who have lived all their lives near water inhabited by roach have never seen one take a natural fly. But there are occasions when they will take a fly if it is offered to them, and I have seen a really wild rise of these fish when the flying-ants were hatching in late summer. It is usual to fish for roach with the fly in fairly shallow water; but, if they should be seen to be rising in the pools good sport may be had by putting before them a reasonable resemblance to the fly they are taking. In this connection I have found the Alder a very good substitute for the flying-ant.

Neither can perch be always relied upon to rise to the fly. But it is a method well worth trying if the fish are seen cruising around near the surface under bushes. Under such conditions it sometimes happens that they will rise very freely and, being very strong fighters, will provide plenty of excitement on the light tackle necessary. The flies for perch should be on the large side and mounted on proportionately large hooks; a small hook tears away almost at once from the mouth of a perch. A boat is nearly always necessary for this style of fishing, and the angler should get a friend to row him along within casting distance of overhanging bushes, pausing before each likely spot to enable him to try it out.

Fly-fishing for pike can scarcely be called serious fishing. The fly itself is usually of such monstrous proportions (the eye part of the feather of a peacock often being used as the wing) that it is certain the fish does not recognise it as any sort of insect. In all probability it is mistaken for a small bird. In some of the Irish lakes pike are taken fairly frequently by means of these enormous flies; but I think the method can be regarded rather as a form of experiment than as a serious method of fishing.

From what I have written on this subject it must not be supposed that the flies I have mentioned are the only flies by which coarse fish may be taken. Far from it. They will take just as many different varieties as trout. But I personally place far more reliance on the presentation of the fly than on the fly itself. Provided the fly has a good shape and will float well I believe it rarely makes any difference what it is supposed to represent. But it does make a great deal of difference if it is not presented to the fish in an attractive manner. By all means try others I have not mentioned and it is always a good plan to obtain a little local knowledge in such matters.

For those who must have a good selection of flies in their box, here are a few more which have proved their worth:

Coachman (for evening work), Red Palmer, Wickham's Fancy, Zulu, Sedge and Hardy's Favourite. A few each of these in three different sizes should be sufficient for anyone.

Chapter V

PIKE

EQUIPMENT

In suggesting the outfit required for pike fishing, let me say at once that I do not consider the equipment for thread-line fishing suitable. It is recommended that the use of this very light rod, fine line and baits which travel close to the surface enables one to spin over weed beds, which it would be almost impossible to do with relatively heavy baits and the old-style rod and reel. But why should one wish to fish for pike above weed beds? It is during the summer or early autumn that pike lie in such situations. They are not then in condition and rarely give any display of their strength. The proper time to start pike fishing is when the first frosts of winter have rotted the weeds. Then, and not before, the pike begin to get into fighting form.

But maybe one wishes to kill pike because they are in water devoted to trout. In this case the summer is as good a time as any other, and at this time of the year they are often easily spotted. For this type of work there is a good selection

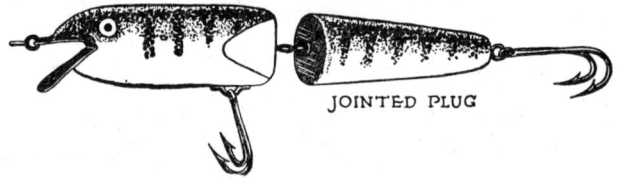
JOINTED PLUG

of light rods, fairly stiff in action, suitable for spinning with light wood plug-baits, of which latter I have found the jointed variety particularly effective. There is also a very wide range of reels, either of the fixed-spool type, or multipliers, or the aerial type. Some of these are so full of gadgets that a new-comer to them must concentrate chiefly on their manipulation rather than on the fishing if he wishes to avoid a complete mix-up. For good straightforward light casting the aerial-type of reel is hard to beat; but there are some equally good multipliers made.

In choosing a rod it should not be forgotten that what may be just the thing for spinning from a boat may be the very reverse when one has to fish from a bank. In a boat a long rod is often a real inconvenience; on the bank a short rod is often completely useless. If you may be fishing at times in either condition, it is safest to buy two rods, one long and the other short, and in this case let the short one be really short—not more than seven feet.

The line should be of plaited silk or flax. In my opinion it is quite unnecessary to have it dressed. In any case it should be dried carefully after use as, if it is dressed, the dressing is liable to wear off when the line is in frequent use. One hundred yards should be ample and the weight should be suited to the reel selected and to the probable weight of the fish you expect to catch.

There are so many varieties of plugs, runts and wrigglers that it would be a waste of time to list them. I doubt if there is much to choose between any of them. The jointed I have already mentioned; another very good pattern is the Hardy " Jock Scott " Wriggler. This bait has the tail triangle kept in

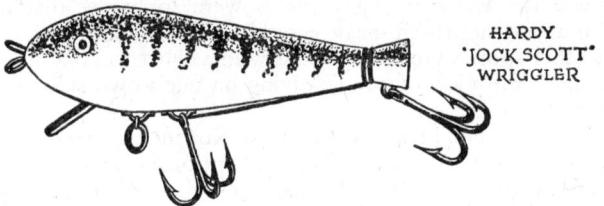

HARDY 'JOCK SCOTT' WRIGGLER

place by means of a turn of thin wire, or a piece of cotton, tied round the tail. When a pike takes this bait the jerk of the strike breaks the wire or cotton and the bait then hangs clear of the pike's mouth so that the fish cannot possibly use it as a lever to free itself from the hooks.

I believe that the complaints one frequently hears that pike are poor fighters may be due to two causes. Many fish are taken during the summer months when they are in a lethargic condition and have little inclination for fighting, and many are taken by means which gives them nothing to fight against. From time to time one hears of large pike up to twenty pounds taken on roach tackle. It is perfectly obvious that these fish did not fight. The angler, knowing full well that his only chance of landing the fish was to keep quiet and calm, and to put no pressure on it, followed this course and eventually coaxed the creature within reach of the gaff or landing net. Pike are rather stupid fish and, if not frightened, they will allow themselves to be towed quietly along without making any resistance; but, if they are given something to fight against, or are in any way frightened, they can usually be depended upon to give a good account of themselves. It is because of this that I favour neither summer pike fishing nor the use of light casting tackle.

The rod I prefer is either of whole bamboo with a greenheart top, or a greenheart butt with split-bamboo middle and top joints. It should have two top joints of different lengths, one to make a relatively short rod for use when fishing from a boat, and the other to make up into a total length of at least twelve feet. In my own case I could not find a rod of the right type long enough to satisfy me, so I made myself an extra long top. I did this because I often fished in a river where the banks in many places were so boggy that one could not approach near enough with a short rod, and in other spots were so high that with a short rod one had to stand in full view of any fish lying on one's own side of the river.

The reel should be the old-type Nottingham wood reel, with a diameter of four inches, and optional check and a line guard. This is a pattern that has stood the test of over half a century and, in my opinion, has never been beaten. A salmon spinning reel will, of course, do excellently, but it is an expensive luxury.

The line should be of plaited silk or flax and can be heavier than that used for the lighter type of reel and rod previously mentioned. It should be remembered that the heavier the line the harder it is to cast.

COARSE FISHING 63

For trace I use a "Tiger" of bronze-finished wire with a breaking strain of twenty to thirty pounds.

My own favourites in spinning baits are the plain "Spoon", the "Colorado", the "Clipper" and the "Wagtail". The "Colorado" and the "Clipper" both have red wool tassels over the tail triangle. These should be squeezed out and

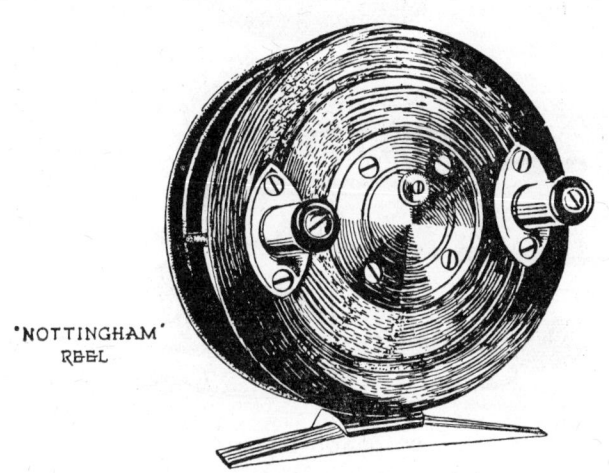

'NOTTINGHAM' REEL

carefully dried on return from the day's fishing, otherwise they will soon rust the hook. There are an enormous number of different designs in artificial baits; but I have found these four quite enough to choose from.

Both the "Colorado" and the "Clipper" have in themselves enough weight to get them down under ordinary circumstances; but the ordinary "Spoon" and the "Wagtail" both require assistance by having weights attached to the trace. The best of all leads for this purpose are the "Jardine" spiral, or grooved leads. They are made in different sizes and can be attached and removed from the trace without interfering with the set-up of the tackle. "Slip-on" anti-kink leads, specially designed for use when spinning, are very useful.

Some anglers prefer to use dead natural baits or pickled

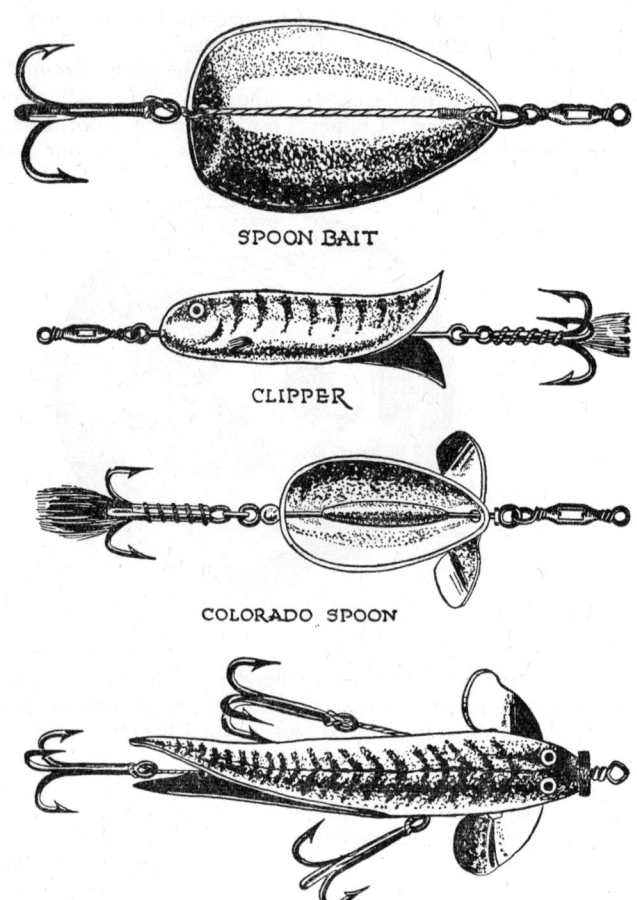

SPOON BAIT

CLIPPER

COLORADO SPOON

WAGTAIL

baits for spinning instead of the manufactured artificials. Two good types of mounts for these preserved, or dead, baits are the "Archer" and the "Lee-Lock". Both of these have "fins" at the head to drive the bait into the required

COARSE FISHING

spin. A very simple mount, which can be made at home, consists of two, or three, triangles, one behind the other, and a single movable lip-hook. The spin in this case is caused by bending the tail of the bait.

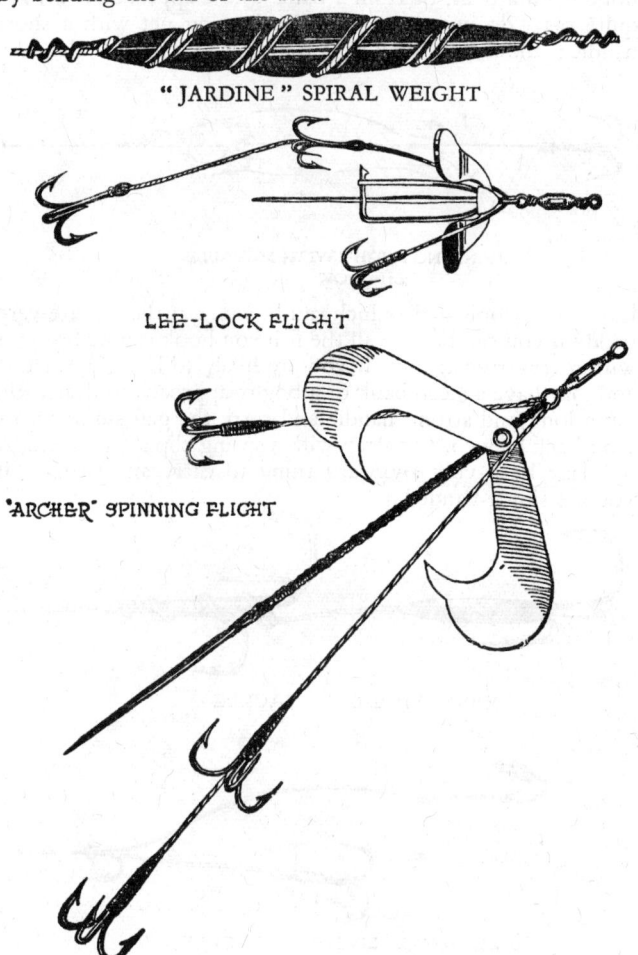

"JARDINE" SPIRAL WEIGHT

LEE-LOCK FLIGHT

'ARCHER' SPINNING FLIGHT

If your net is not deep and has not a very wide mouth you will require either a gaff or a net sufficiently large to take a fish of twenty pounds. Unless all your pike fishing is to be done from a boat, or from a bank where approach is always quite easy, do not get a gaff or a landing net with a short handle; the handle should be four feet in length at the very

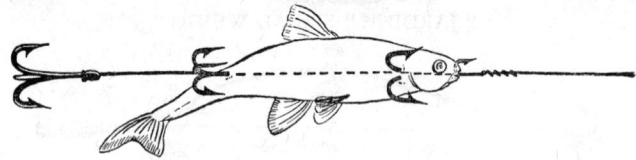

SPINNING FLIGHT WITH MOVABLE LIPHOOK

least. Telescopic gaffs which can be hung at the hip are very handy if you can be sure all the fish you hook can be brought within easy reach; but, if you are likely to be fishing alone and may have a steep bank or a boggy approach to deal with, get a long and strong handle and carry the gaff slung across your back by a cord or strap with a spring clip attachment. A net may be a very awkward thing to carry and manage if you are single-handed.

'JARDINE' LIVE-BAIT TACKLE

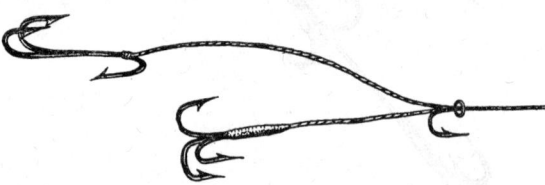

'BICKERDYKE' LIVE-BAIT TACKLE

COARSE FISHING

For fishing with a live-bait you will require special hooks and, in most cases, special floats. Of the various flights of hooks designed to carry live-baits the "Jardine" and "Bickerdyke" are probably the most popular. An improvement on these, in that it requires the insertion of only one hook in the bait, is the "Mullins" snap tackle. In this case

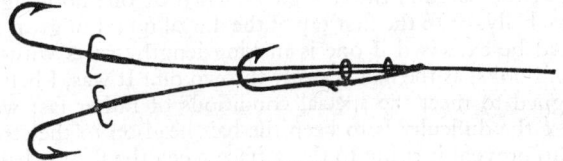

"MULLINS" SNAP TACKLE

CAPTAIN PARKER'S SNAP TACKLE

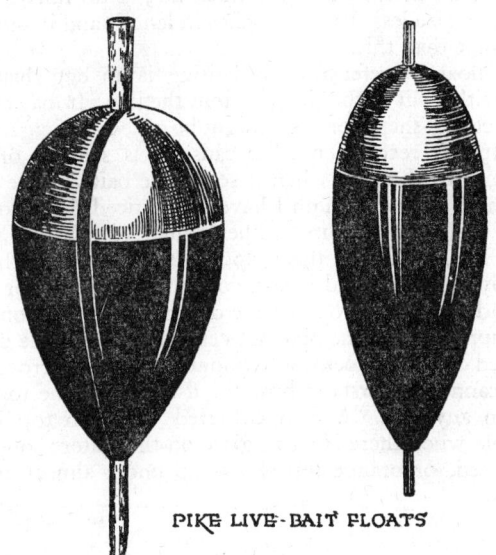

PIKE LIVE-BAIT FLOATS

the side hooks are secured to the sides of the bait by means of a rubber-band passing under the belly. A recent and excellent development of the snap tackle is that designed by Captain L. A. Parker, of Downton, near Salisbury. This consists of a single triangle and a movable lip-hook. The lip-hook is passed either through one (the upper), or both lips, of the bait and the triangle attached by one hook lightly to the belly, or to the first ray of the dorsal fin; but great care should be exercised if one is making lengthy casts with this set of hooks, as the bait is easily thrown off. It was, I believe, designed to meet the special conditions of rather fast water where the difficulty is to keep the bait head-on to the stream and to prevent it rising to the surface when the float is halted.

The use of live-bait necessitates the use of a pail or live-bait can unless one is fishing from a boat which has a live-bait well. The can should be roomy; but it should not be overlooked that the more water you have to carry the heavier it will be. There is nothing I have seen better than the oblong zinc kettle with perforated lid; I do not think it is made in a size less than ten inches in length and it should not be smaller than this.

The float I prefer for live-baiting is an egg-shaped one made with a slit in the side to admit the line. It may either be a perfect egg-shape, or what might be called a fat cigar-shape; the latter is recommended because it is said to offer less resistance to the pike when it seizes the bait. There may be something in this, though I have not noticed that pike object to the resistance set up by the regular egg-shaped style of float. But, whatever the shape of the float, see that it is brightly coloured (and if not, colour it yourself), for it must be clearly visible to you at some distance under all conditions. It is supposed that the pike notices the colour of the float and is scared off if this does not harmonise with the surroundings; but I cannot understand how the fish can see the top of the float in any case. A float coloured white on top is often invisible when there is a sun-glare on the water; one with a black, red, or orange top shows up under almost any conditions.

Chapter VI

COARSE FISHING

SPINNING FOR PIKE

The best pike-spinning is to be had during the winter months when frosts have cleared most of the weeds out of the water, or at any rate rendered them so rotten that a pike plunging into them rarely gets so firmly fixed that it cannot be coaxed free. Furthermore, it is not until the weather begins to get cold, with frosts at night, that pike get into fighting trim. But, since (in most waters) the season opens in the middle of June, with that of other coarse fish, some description of the methods to be followed at this time of the year are to be expected.

Since it is chiefly during the summer months that one may expect to find pike near the surface (or in relatively shallow water, which amounts to much the same thing), it is at this time of the year that thread-line fishing may be employed with success. I do not wish to imply that pike cannot be taken in winter by this method; but, since it is almost impossible to fish in this style at any great depth, it follows that it is most appropriate to that time of the year when pike may be expected to be within reach of it. It is also during the summer that pike frequently lie just beneath the tops of weed beds or even just above the tops, and it is then that they may be fished for by the thread-line method with the bait travelling just above the weeds. In connection with this it may be as well to point out that these light plug baits used in the thread-line method of fishing do not spin. They wag and wobble in a most life-like manner, but they do not revolve. In spite of this their use has been generally accepted as coming under the heading of spinning.

Pike are most likely to be found near the surface during the early morning or at dusk, and it is therefore at these hours that it is usually profitable to fish for them by the thread-line method during the summer months. A good plan is to be rowed slowly along in a boat over the likely spots. When a pike is hooked over weeds it invariably plunges into them, or attempts to do so. When one is fishing from a boat it is, of course, very much easier to free a weed-entangled pike than when one is confined to the bank. In most cases the pike caught by this method at this time of the year are not large, in my experience rarely exceeding five pounds.

Not only should one fish above the weeds and in the relatively shallower parts of the water, but outside rush beds and where belts of flags or reeds grow from the water are also spots which should not be neglected. Pike love to lie handy to such places where they are hidden from sight by reason of their close resemblance to the bands of light and shadow of the plants and from which they can dart out at their prey. As nearly as possible the bait should be made to travel within a couple of feet of such spots and parallel to them.

One should make up one's mind before starting to fish whether one wishes to kill the pike or return them uninjured to the water. Though pike can be gaffed without being damaged in the slightest, a big net is safer in the hands of an assistant or even in the hands of the angler if he is not quite familiar with the use of the gaff. There is little need to describe how a pike should be netted except to say that the fish should be brought to the net, not the net to the fish, and to point out that a great many lightly-hooked fish have been knocked off by an incautious lunge with the landing net. If you wish to land a pike uninjured by means of the gaff, slip the point into the opening of the gills and lift with the handle of the gaff held upright. If the fish is to be killed I always either hook it with the gaff right under the chin with a quick jerk directly upwards, or strike over the pike's shoulder so that the gaff enters behind the gills. I have heard it said that a pike should be gaffed in the tail so that it is unable to thrash about whilst being lifted out; as I have always followed the other method with success I have never attempted to gaff one in the tail myself and imagine it cannot be so very easy.

I have landed a number of pike by gripping them between finger and thumb below the eyelids. There is a hard, bony ridge above a pike's eyes and a very firm grip can be taken by

COARSE FISHING

putting finger and thumb into the eye-sockets; it is a much safer method of carrying than inserting the fingers into the gills, where they may easily become damaged and perhaps poisoned by contact with the sharp little spines on the gill arches.

As soon as the leaves are off the trees is the time to take up serious pike fishing, and I should certainly recommend spinning in favour of any other method. It is often claimed that the largest pike are taken only by the use of a live-bait; but this statement is not confirmed by the records. Many of the largest pike have been taken by spinning and it is probably true to say that far more would be taken by this means were it practised more frequently. I think that the reason why so many anglers rarely spin for pike is because it may become a relatively expensive hobby. One is very much more likely to lose one's tackle when spinning than when live-baiting, and it does not take many artificial baits and wire traces lost to make your fishing an expensive pastime.

I have recommended a longer rod than is usual for pike-spinning, in spite of the fact that it is very much more tiring to use a long rod than a short one. But I consider that in most cases the advantages of the longer rod outweigh its disadvantages. Many anglers fail to realise how very conspicuous they must be standing silhouetted against the sky on top of the high bank of the river. The pike is just as wary as any other fish and has quite as good eyesight as the others. To say that he is a ravenous fish does not mean that he is without caution. As a matter of fact he is no more ravenous than any other fish and will often go for days without attempting to feed. A good many years ago I fished, with two others, every afternoon for a week over the same half-mile of water. All three of us were spinning and we varied our baits from time to time when we thought the pike were not interested in what we happened to be showing them. In the six consecutive days on which we fished we did not average more than one sizeable pike between the three of us each day. The other two declared that there could be very few pike in the stretch; but I, who lived on the spot, was quite sure that there were plenty, and that they had only to keep at it to strike the lucky day. The following Monday my two friends turned up again soon after two o'clock for another afternoon after pike. I could not join them as I had other work on hand. They called on me before half past four, each carrying a couple of good pike, and declared that they had never known anything like it. From the start the pike had run at their baits at almost every cast. Between them they had returned over double numbers alive to the river, a good many of which they would have retained under ordinary circumstances. They declared that there must have been literally scores of pike in that short stretch.

If you come to a pool with a steep bank, look first to see if there is a place where you can get down close to the water with safety. Fish from there if at all possible. Failing this, look for a bush which will give you a background against the sky. The bush may be rather an inconvenience to you when casting; but it is better to be inconvenienced a little and catch fish, than to have all the freedom of wide meadows behind you and catch nothing. And, if you cannot get close to the water under the bank and cannot find a bush to cover you against the sky, keep both rod and yourself as low as possible and as far away from the bank of the river as possible. It is under such circumstances that you will find out how great a help a long rod can be.

I assume that you are fishing with a Nottingham reel fitted with line-guard and optional check, and that you have mounted a " tiger " trace weighted suitably to the water and ending with your favourite artificial bait. You should be able to cast either from the right- or left-hand side as appears to be most convenient under the circumstances. With the top of the rod held about level with the top of your own head you stand with your left shoulder facing the stream and your rod parallel to the river bank. Remove the check from the reel, swing the bait steadily forward and then back again, with a slight upward movement of the rod top as the bait reaches the extremity of its swing in both cases. Then, as the bait swings forward once again, give it a further strong influence from the rod and let it fly straight out over the water. During these movements your right hand will be gripping the rod above the reel, and your left will be below the reel with the edge of the first finger almost touching the rim of the reel. Watching the flight of the bait you will hold the first finger of the left hand in readiness to apply its edge gently to the revolving edge of the reel, if necessary, in order to steady down the flight of the bait and cause it to fall just clear of the weeds along the other bank rather than just

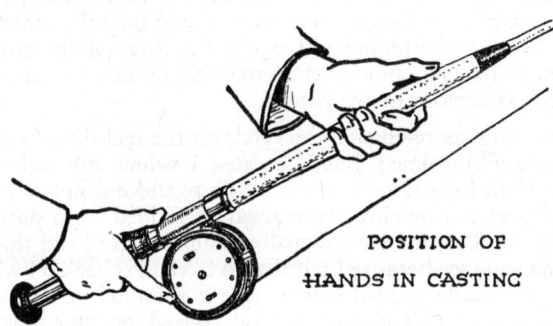

POSITION OF HANDS IN CASTING

beyond the single strand of barbed-wire stretched there to keep the bullocks from getting into the river—it is most vexing to have to decide whether it is better to save expense by walking a mile to the nearest bridge, going down the other bank of the river, releasing your bait, putting it into the water (or much more wisely removing it and carrying it with you), walking back round the bridge again—which in all will occupy nearly an hour; or saving time at the cost of a perfectly good trace, weight and spinning-bait, by breaking. With careful practice one can achieve great accuracy and the casting itself may become such an absorbing occupation that a fish suddenly taking the bait may come as a quite unexpected and almost alarming shock. The position of the hands is reversed when the cast is made from the right side of the body.

After the cast the bait should be given a moment or two to allow it to sink as far as one considers it safe and should then be recovered by turning the handle of the reel slowly. With most people, the left hand holds the rod above the reel and the right does the turning. The actual speed must depend on the force of the current, remembering that you will be much more likely to take the large pike if you spin deeply and slowly, than if you make your bait travel high and fast through the water. In quite dead water the bait will not spin unless it is travelling at sufficient speed to keep it horizontal; but in fast water, such as that coming out from under a hatch, the bait can be actually held in one spot, where it will revolve swiftly and prove very attractive to the pike which is quite likely to be hiding just where the force of the stream passes the patch of almost still water behind the wall supporting the framework of the hatch.

Some anglers re-engage the catch on the reel directly they start recovering line; but I, because I valued my reel very much when I obtained it as a schoolboy and did not wish to wear it out too quickly, have always refrained from putting on the check until I have actually struck a fish. I did this in the first instance because I felt that to have the check on when it was not really needed was to give it a lot of unnecessary wear and tear. Whichever method you adopt, you must at any rate have the check on whilst playing a fish, or you may very soon get everything in a very bad tangle.

Pike frequently lie along the banks of streams, very often actually under them, for many river banks are undercut in places, though it may be to a depth of only a few inches. Because pike so frequently lie quite close to the banks, it follows that you are often more likely to get a run from one close to the bank than in any other part. You can do little to control the course of the bait as it leaves the neighbourhood of the opposite bank of the river; but you can do a great deal to control it as it reaches your own bank. Keep it spinning just clear of the weeds and just off the bank for as long a distance as possible. And keep back from the bank yourself or you will often have the mortification of seeing a good fish turn away with a flash because it has caught sight of you just as it was about to take the bait.

Alongside reed beds, under overhanging bushes and just inside side bays are all excellent spots in which to find pike. They are also very likely to be found just where meadow drains and ditches join the main stream, or where two streams join.

As with a good many other types of fish, there are certain pools which seem always to attract the larger specimens of pike. Again and again you will hear that the largest fish for the season was taken in one of perhaps three recognised haunts. Except that these places usually conform to one or other of the types of favourite spots I have described, you can do little to recognise them and must rely on your own experience or powers of observation. If you can obtain the help of a local angler, so much the better.

Towards the latter end of the season it always pays to devote a good deal of attention to spots in the neighbourhood of ditches or quiet side bays. It is to these spots that most of the pike will retire for spawning, and it is somewhere near them that you will be likely to find the fish as the spawning season draws near.

In ponds and lakes pike often spawn in quite shallow water; in fact, I do not believe that they ever spawn in really deep water; so it should be towards these shallower spots that you should make your way when fishing in late February or early March and, should you take a good fish, continue to spin all around that spot for some time, for it is more than likely that its companion will be close at hand. Very many times, when spinning during the latter part of the pike fishing season, I have taken the second fish from almost exactly the same spot as the first within five minutes of getting the other on to the bank.

The best artificial bait to use is that in which you have most confidence, which is most frequently in use, and which is fished in the most attractive manner.

Chapter VII

LIVE-BAITING

The first consideration in setting out to fish for pike with a live-bait is to have a rod which is capable of casting a bait weighing five or six ounces a distance of twenty or thirty yards, and also capable of driving the hooks home into the bony jaws of the fish when it takes hold. As to the length, that is a matter of opinion; for my own part I prefer a rod of at least ten feet. The longer the rod the easier it is to cast and the easier it is to guide a fish clear of weed beds. With such a rod also one can reach out to fish over riverside herbage and fish beyond weed beds. A steel-centred rod is the strongest and the most capable of driving the hooks in; but it is more expensive than the bamboo or cane rod. The rod should have the largest rings it can carry and they should be lined either with agate or porcelain. I doubt if there is anything to choose between the two materials; it seems to be largely a question of price.

Of reels there is an enormous choice and I think the most important point to insist on is that they should have wide drums. My own is the same wooden "Nottingham" reel I use for spinning. It has never let me down. In years of use the only repair that has been needed was a new check spring. But I think one is really safer with one not made entirely of wood. My own has never warped; but I know of others which have. There are now "Nottingham" reels made of vulcanite and various metal alloys; there are also reels of the same type made of wood and metal, the metal being in the inner plate as well as the fittings. But whatever one decides upon with regard to rod, reel, line and hooks, make quite sure that they fit each other and the type of pike you are likely to meet with. To fish with heavy tackle on a light rod is asking for trouble, and so also is it an almost certain prelude to disappointment to use light tackle and small hooks with a rod of considerable weight and strength.

The line should be dressed with some such preparation such as "Mucilin" and, though it need not be a "dressed" line, it will help to keep the water out of it and, therefore, help to keep a line afloat that is soaked in linseed oil.

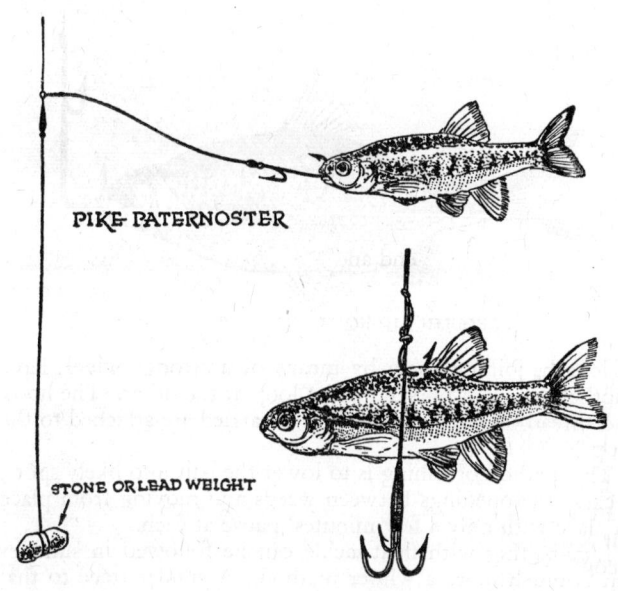

The two usual methods of live-baiting are either by means of the paternoster or by using float and snap tackle.

The paternoster I consider essentially a summer method of live-baiting. In its simplest form it may consist of a yard of gut substitute with a hook at the end and a suitable weight attached to the hook loop by means of a length of thread, or fine string. The idea of having the lead attached by thread or string is so that it may break free should it foul a sunken branch or other obstruction. The hook may be either a simple large lip-hook, or the double " Raboulin " lip-hook, consisting of a smaller upper hook set at right-angles to the lip-hook, or one of the already mentioned snap tackles. A rather better type of paternoster can be made by taking two lengths of bronzed steel, or alloy wire, each eighteen inches

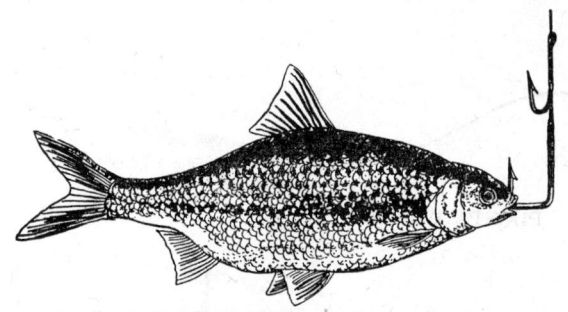

'RABOULIN' LIP-HOOK

in length, joining them by means of a strong swivel; have another swivel at one end and a loop at the other. The hook and thread on which the weight is carried are attached to the loop.

The method of fishing is to lower the bait into likely spot , such as the openings between weeds and moving from place to place with only a few minutes' pause at each.

Live-baiting with float-tackle can be followed in summer but is much more a winter method. A similar trace to that recommended for paternoster fishing is required; but in this case only the bait-hook is attached to the bottom end, the weight being fixed above the middle swivel. The weight may be a bored " Barleycorn ", in which case it is made up in the trace; but I prefer to add a " Jardine " grooved weight after the trace has been built up.

The main float, for which I prefer the " Fishing Gazette " float, an egg-shaped cork with a slit in the side for admission of the line, must be of such a size as will carry the bait, but no more. The very large floats sometimes used will often cause pike to leave the bait when they feel such a drag against them. It is generally advisable to add a couple of pilot floats

COARSE FISHING

to prevent the line sinking and becoming twisted round beneath the float. I use a small bung cut in half with holes bored wide enough to allow the line to pass with perfect freedom.

The hooks may be either of the snap tackles already referred to; or, if only a small bait is used, a simple triangle with one of its hooks slipped under the dorsal fin of the bait.

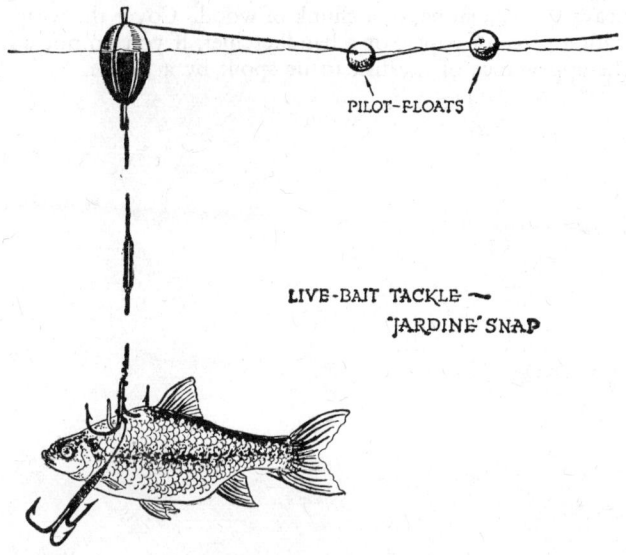

LIVE-BAIT TACKLE — "JARDINE" SNAP

There is some difference of opinion regarding the best method of striking a pike and the best time to do it. But on one point most pike anglers are agreed, that with single hook tackle one should give the fish a little longer time than with snap tackle; but even with snap tackle a few moments should be given to allow the pike to get the bait well inside its mouth, particularly if the bait is on the large side. The strike itself should be decisive, but not necessarily a sudden violent heave. My own method, which is quite successful, is to pick up the slack line when I am preparing to strike and, directly

I feel the fish, give a quick, steady pull and hold it for a second or two. The most effective moment at which to strike is when the pike is actually moving away. The strike should, of course, then be in the opposite direction to that in which the pike is going.

To kill a pike it should be given a sharp rap with an object above and slightly behind the eyes. A " priest " may be carried for this purpose, or one may use the butt of a heavy knife, a stone, or a chunk of wood. Cover the weapon with a piece of paper, or a handkerchief, if you do not want the appearance of the fish to be spoilt by a bruise.

PART III

SEA FISHING

Chapter VIII

SEA FISHING

EQUIPMENT

THE coarse fish angler who decides to take up sea angling will already have some equipment suitable for certain forms of the latter. His pike rod will probably serve for either boat- or shore-fishing, or for fishing from rocks and piers; his pike reel may also serve for both; and so may his pike line. Some of his hooks, weights, gut substitute, traces and floats may also come in handy. For boat-fishing he will be able to use his pike rod with its shortest top, and for use from the shore or rocks the same rod with its longest top joint will probably answer quite well. With regard to hooks and any form of his equipment made of metal, he will have to remember that salt water rusts steel very much quicker than fresh water and he must, therefore, be very careful to wash all metal parts of his tackle in fresh water after an outing, dry it thoroughly and give it a coating of oil, vaseline, or some similar grease.

The question of a suitable rod will depend very largely on the amount of weight it will have to carry. In some spots, where very heavy tides run, very heavy weights have to be used to get the bait down to the fish and keep it there. A light pike rod would be most unsuitable for this type of fishing. And the same applies to both reels and lines.

If the angler contemplates going in for such heavy fish as tope or tunny he will certainly have to have special rods for the purpose. These Big Fish rods are usually made in two pieces, a butt and a long, single joint. They may be of greenheart, or built split-cane, the latter, of course, being the stronger and more expensive. As these rods have nothing to support the main joint when taken down for travelling, it is essential that they should be provided with a strong wood or metal case. The simplest form of case, and one which can be made at home, is made by joining two lengths of wood along their longest sides so that they stand at right-angles to each other and finishing off by fixing a triangle of wood to each end. Such a case should be made large enough to take two rods. I have taken as many as four in my own, when I have been going to a new district and have only a very hazy idea of what

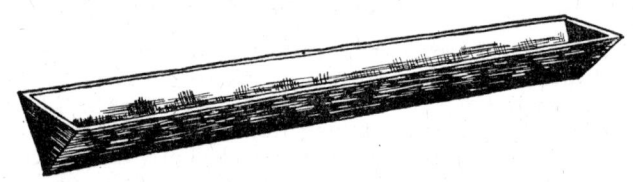

SIMPLE ROD CASE

type of fish I may be likely to find there; in this case the additional rods are packed on top of the others and the whole bundle well wrapped in brown paper and tied securely down its whole length with strong string. I consider this method better than using a rod-box, which cannot possibly carry more than a limited number of rods, though the resulting parcel may not be quite so neat in appearance.

There are some very good sea rods made in three joints with two spare tops of different lengths. When fitted with the longest top they measure just over ten feet. The tops are made of greenheart and the two bottom joints of whole cane, and they are fitted with strong non-rusting rings, porcelain butt and end rings, rubber button and rustless reel fittings. They are strong and relatively cheap, and for general sea rods covering most ordinary purposes are, in my opinion, quite the best type of rod to have.

If very heavy weights have to be cast it is advisable to use a rod specially built for the purpose. These extra strong rods are made of selected split cane, are fitted with specially strong ferrules and rings, and have steel centres. They will stand up to very severe strains. But, of course, the best of them are rather expensive.

A trout fly-rod will also come in useful at times, but this need not be one bought specially for the purpose, or, if it is, it should be the cheapest obtainable provided it is reasonably strong. An old trout spinning rod would be just the thing.

The reel should be made either of bakelite or wood, and as a general-purpose sea reel I should recommend one fitted

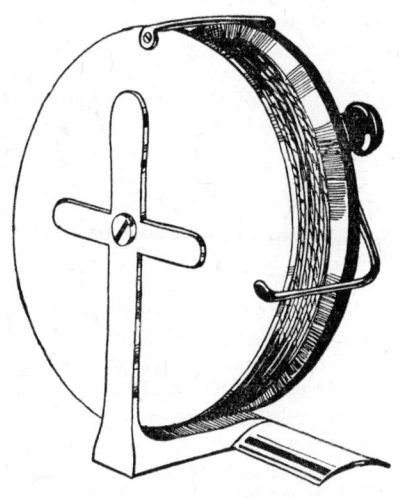

"COLONIAL" REEL

with a check and line guard, and with a diameter of at least four inches. Such a reel as the "Aerialite", made of bakelite with non-corrosive fittings is a very good type; or for heavier work one such as the "Colonial", which has a heavy star-back support of brass and is fitted with an adjustable drag and line guard, is quite suitable. On no account should one make the mistake of buying a cheap sea reel, the sort which are intended to catch schoolboys on holiday with a few extra shillings pocket money to spend. The reel has to stand up to much more strain in sea-fishing than it does in freshwater-fishing, and a good article, looked after carefully, will suffer a great deal of heavy work over a great many years and be little the worse for it.

For spinning or long-distance casting I know of no better reel than the "Scarborough". The best of these are fitted with an adjustable tension so that one may regulate them to the weight used and so minimise the risk of overruns.

With regard to lines, one must remember at the start that lines used for sea-fishing deteriorate very much more rapidly than when used for freshwater-fishing. The line should always be dried carefully after use and it is a good plan first to soak the part used in a basin of fresh water before hanging it up to dry. But see that the line is as strong as will fit the rod. One hundred yards is enough for all ordinary purposes; but, if the angler contemplates a visit to one of the Western Ireland fishing grounds, say, where he may get hold of something outsize, it would be advisable to have two hundred yards. It should be made of plaited flax and should be "waterproofed". I like to feel that I am on the safe side and so use a line of from forty to fifty pounds breaking strain. This may sound excessive when one expects no more than an occasional ten-pound fish; but it must be remembered that the line grows gradually weaker throughout its life and there is always the possibility that one may have to deal with such fish as very heavy conger or halibut. A good strong line such as I have suggested will answer well for all general purposes; a lighter or heavier line being purchased if later on one wishes to go in for lighter or heavier styles of fishing.

For traces of all types there is nothing that will do so well as gut substitute; a couple of coils of about forty yards each and in two thicknesses, "heavy trout" and "sea", will serve almost any occasion. It is cheap, wears well and, until it begins to turn white, which it does after some use, it is nearly invisible in the water. It is economical to discard it as soon as it starts fraying and fading, the cost of six feet being merely a matter of a few pence.

With regard to hooks, which, of course, must be sea hooks, specially treated to withstand the corrosion of salt water, I like to keep a selection; some loose and eyed, and others bought already attached to gut lengths. Some sea-anglers do not believe in buying hooks ready made-up on gut lengths; but I have not yet heard a convincing argument against the practice. It sometimes happens that one must put up one's tackle at the greatest possible speed in order to catch the tide at some particular state, such as the second hour of the flow. Any minutes saved under these conditions may make a considerable difference to the bag. I prefer a round

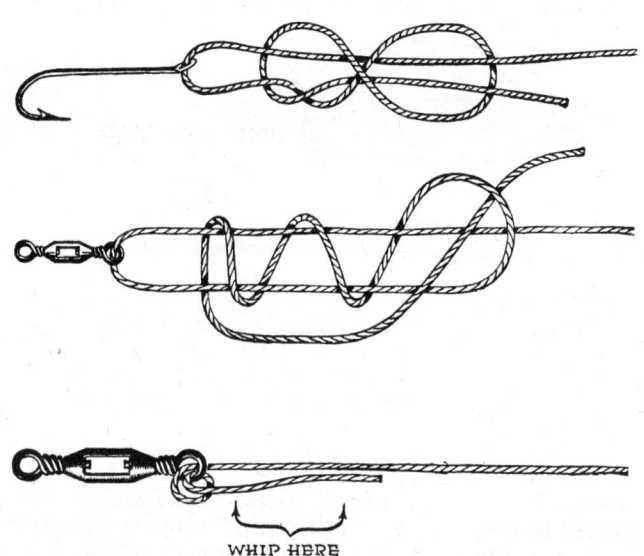

WHIP HERE

or Limerick bend hook and the size must, of course, depend on the size of the bait one happens to be using. When attaching hooks to gut substitute the latter should first be well soaked. The knot must be one which will neither slip nor cut, the one illustrated being reliable.

In making up traces I often use simply a double over-hand knot. This holds, though it does not look very neat. A much neater knot is figured. If I make up my tackle well beforehand, I whip all the joins with waxed silk and varnish afterwards, usually passing the gut twice through swivel rings to lessen friction.

It is essential when buying swivels to avoid those made of steel, as anything made of steel quickly rusts in salt water.

For heavy fish, such as large conger, it is advisable to be provided with some rustless steel or phosphor bronze wire traces with swivels and hook attached; and even these, though they are supposed to be rustless, should be washed in fresh water after use and given a rub over with oil.

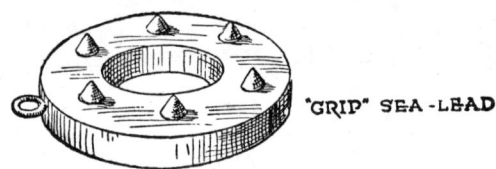

"GRIP" SEA-LEAD

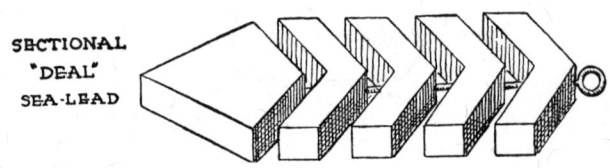

SECTIONAL "DEAL" SEA-LEAD

There are a good many types of leads used in various methods of sea-fishing, some of which run to a pound in weight. I always carry a few "Jardine" spiral weights, some pierced bullets, and one or two "grip" sea leads. The latter are lead rings with small blunt points around the flat surfaces of the circle and can be obtained in different weights. A very useful weight is the sectional "Deal" weight which is so made that you can add to, or substract from, the total weight by putting on, or removing the sections.

A gaff will be necessary if you are fishing for heavy fish, or even if you expect only to get fish of a few pounds in weight. It is better to get this made by a blacksmith: or, if you may be fishing from rocks as well as from a boat, get him to make two. The metal should be mild steel, the point should be three to four inches long, and the gape should not exceed two and a half inches—you may have to gaff a conger and this will be a most difficult operation if you have a gaff with a wide gape. The gaff for use in a boat should be lashed with copper wire and stout tanned water cord to a broom-handle about three feet long. The gaff for use from rocks should have a handle at least five feet long. It is a good plan to screw a wooden button to the end of the gaff handle so that it will not slip through the hands. Some people bore a hole through the end of the handle and make a loop of stout cord

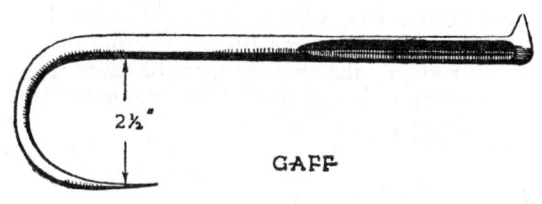

GAFF

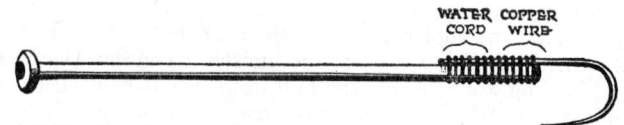

GAFF WITH "BUTTON" ON HANDLE TO PREVENT SLIPPING

through this, which they slip over the wrist. I don't like the idea of having a gaff attached to me in this way; to fall overboard, or slip from the rocks, with a tool like this swinging about one's legs does not seem to me to be wise; but it is a good plan when fishing from a boat to have the gaff tied by a long, strong cord to some part of the boat so that it cannot be lost overboard.

Chapter IX

SEA FISHING

SHORE FISHING

Since I am writing for the general sea angler rather than for the specialist, I propose to start with fishing from the shore, because this is certainly the cheapest form of sea-fishing and also, in its various forms of beach, pier and rock fishing, probably the most popular of all styles.

At its simplest it can be merely a hand-line with a weighted line and baited hook, though this should be termed catching, or attempting to catch, fish rather than angling. A more advanced, but still quite simple form, may be much the same, but with the addition of a rod. The bait will be whatever happens to be available: ragworms, lugworms, mussels, strips of mackerel or herring, sand-eels, or even limpets. Sometimes the angler can buy bait from the local boatmen; at others he must search for it himself. Though mackerel and herring are probably the best dead fish as bait, strips of almost any other sea-fish will often act quite well in this capacity, and even portions of kipper are not to be despised.

Though one does not usually catch such large fish from the shore as from a boat, nor does one usually catch so many, very good sport may often be had by this method of angling. If the angler is a stranger to the district, is a poor sailor, or does not wish to go to the expense of hiring a boat, I would recommend him to rig up his tackle with a " grip " weight at the end and two hooks, one about six inches from the weight and the other three to four feet farther up the cast. The best time to fish will probably be from the start of the flow until about a quarter of the ebb. If he is fishing from a shelving shore and finds the small crabs troublesome, it is often advisable to get right away from the spot and try elsewhere; but if he is fishing in a harbour, or from rocks, he can often get his bait away from them by shifting the lowest hook another foot up the cast and not throwing out so far—in other words, by keeping the line at a steep angle with the rod top he can keep the bait out of the reach of the crabs. He may in this manner obtain good sport with flounders, plaice, eels, and bass, besides several other kinds of fish according to the locality.

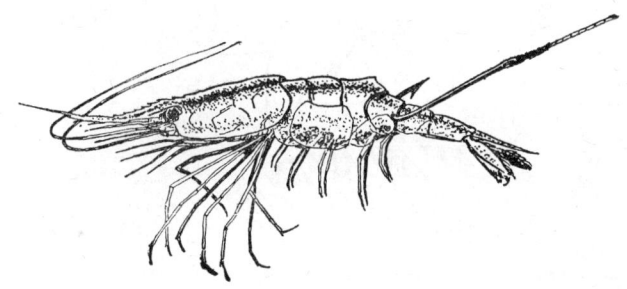

Live shrimps and prawns are often excellent baits for use in this method of angling, and it is sometimes a good plan, if two different kinds of bait can be obtained, to have one kind on one hook and the other on the second hook. Shrimps and prawns should be hooked through the tail. If mackerel or herring is used, the fish should be filleted with a sharp knife and cut into strips with the skin adhering.

One sometimes sees shore anglers using a heavy anchor-weight to keep the tackle in its place. Another dodge is to tie or bolt the ends of two bamboo canes together and with these and the rod form a tripod, so that the rod need not be held in the hand the whole time. I am not in favour of the anchor-weight, as it anchors the fish as well as the bait, with the result that the fish can give no sport whatever: this is merely catching fish. But, as I can see no particular virtue in holding a rod for an indefinite period waiting for a bite, I think the tripod arrangement a very sensible one.

In all places where dabs or flounders may be expected—that is in harbours, estuaries, and where the bottom is sandy or muddy, one hook should be placed below the weight. These fish feed on the bottom and, though occasionally I have taken one on a hook which must have been quite two feet from the bottom, this is rather unusual. The grip weight,

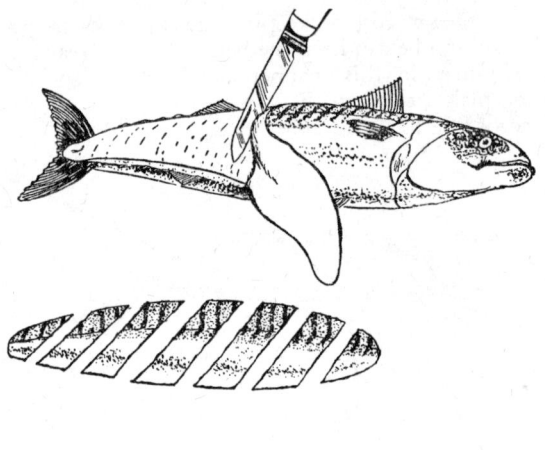

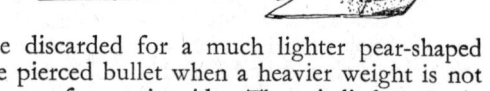

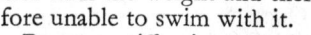

also, should be discarded for a much lighter pear-shaped weight or large pierced bullet when a heavier weight is not needed on account of an easier tide. There is little sport in hauling up fish which are lighter than the weight and therefore unable to swim with it.

ANCHOR WEIGHT

Booms—stiff wire stretchers to keep the hook lengths of gut from fouling the main trace —are often used when fishing from the shore; but I consider them an unnecessary encumbrance. By arranging the hooks paternoster style, that is to say one above the other on the trace, one rarely meets with any difficulties in this direction. I think also that a lot of conspicuous wire about the tackle must warn shy fish not to take liberties with the bait.

In all cases where there are rocks, or even the rubbish of old cycle wheels, etc., often seen about the bottoms of harbours, fasten the lead weight to the tackle by means of fairly fine string, or gut of considerably less strength than that of the trace. In case of a hang-up one then loses only the weight instead of the whole set of tackle.

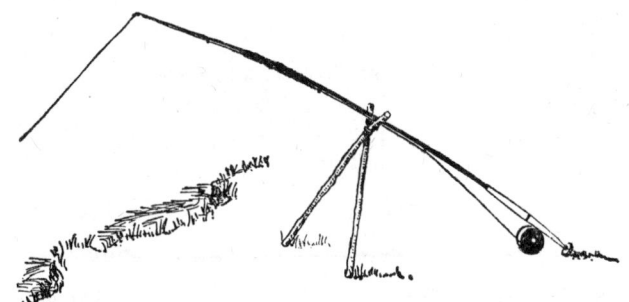

Although short-shanked hooks are sometimes difficult to extract from the fish, they should always be used when fishing for flat fish, except when lugworm is the bait.

A most enjoyable form of fishing for flat fish is by the use of tackle similar to that employed in roach fishing. This cannot well be used where there is much of a tide run; but in stiller water it gives one a chance of appreciating the fighting qualities of these fish. A trout-spinning rod or a rod of similar lightness should be used, and the depth will have to be plumbed from time to time to make sure the bait is on the bottom.

Often the best season for flat fish is from the end of September until the close of the year, or even later. An advantage of this time of the year is that one gets very little trouble with the crabs, which go off into deep water or lay up for the winter as soon as the water begins to get cold. A live shrimp is an excellent bait for flat fish.

Good sport may also be had with other fish by using float-tackle but with a heavier type of float. The tackle should consist of a stout gut substitute trace with one hook at the bottom and another some two feet above, the lead being a spiral "Jardine" of suitable weight and the whole supported by a pike float. If whiting are the fish anticipated the bait should be about two feet from the bottom unless one happens to be fishing at night or at dusk. Whiting often feed quite close to the surface after dark.

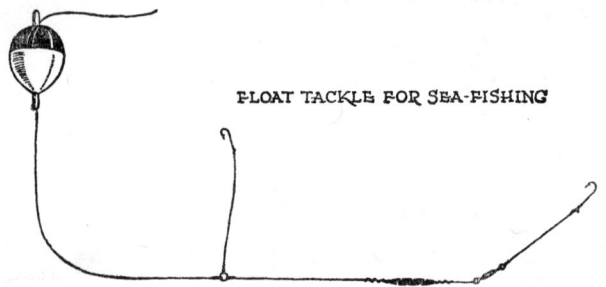

FLOAT TACKLE FOR SEA-FISHING

Similar tackle, but with only one hook and that at the bottom end of the trace, may be used for bass. Bass are mostly found close to rocks or weeds (the two usually going together), and it is inadvisable to use more than one hook when fishing for these strong and fast fighters. The hook may be either a single, a triangle, or a "Mumbles" bass set, depending on the type of bait used. No rule can be laid down for this as it is found that bass differ in their tastes in different localities. In one spot the favourite bait may be ragworm, in another live prawn, in another soft crab. The preference may be for mackerel, herring, pilchard, rather high bloater, lugworm, sand-eel, spinner or rubber sand-eel.

The "Mumbles" tackle is excellent for soft crab. The bait, which may be either the whole crab, or only a part, according to its size, is placed in the loop and pressed on to the two inner hooks, being kept in position by pressing down the tube (A) and so closing the loop.

If a single hook is used with soft crab the bait should be tied on securely. For this purpose darning-wool serves well. The hook should be passed through the crab from beneath and out at the back, and the wool should be tied round in front of the last pair of legs.

If a triangle is used it should be passed right through the crab so that the latter rests in the bends of the three hooks.

A very good tackle which hooks well and from which one does not readily lose the bait is made by lashing two smaller hooks to the shank of a large hook so that they stick out on the opposite side to the large hook. They should be fastened very securely with waxed

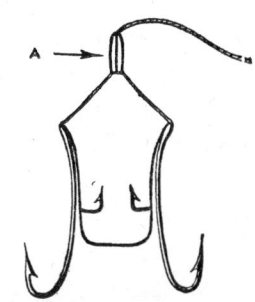

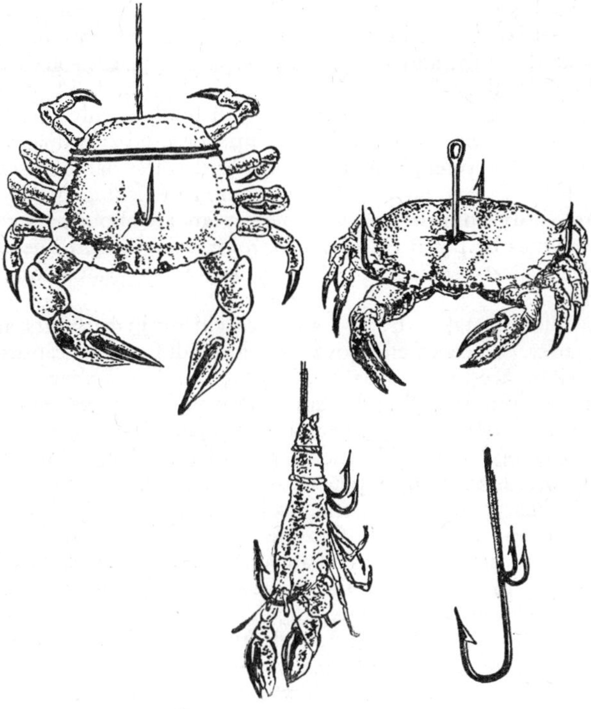

"MUMBLES" BASS TACKLE

thread and varnished. The crab rests in the bend of the large hook and the two smaller hooks are hidden amongst its legs. In this case also the bait should be tied securely to the shank of the hook.

Bass may also be taken by the use of a drift-line with no weight, or in any case only a very light one. A live prawn or

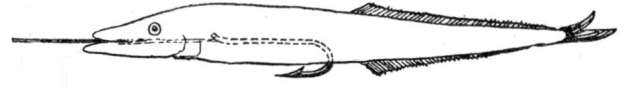

METHOD OF HOOKING SAND-EEL

sand-eel is usually the bait used for this type of fishing. The sand-eel is hooked by passing the hook through its mouth, out at the gills, and fixing it by passing it just through the skin under the fish. This is the recognised method of hooking sand-eels; but they will live longer if hooked only through the lips. An ordinary bottle-cork may be used as a float and this is to be preferred to a real float as it is less liable to scare the fish. In several places this method of fishing produces good sport from the beach. When sprats are about bass may sometimes be taken from the shore by using a drift-line and a dead sprat hooked in the same way as suggested for the sand-eel.

Mullet are taken by rod and line chiefly in harbours and estuaries. They often prove extremely difficult to capture: but there are times, usually when the weather is very warm, when they feed well and seem to lose their extreme shyness. I know of one estuary where a great many fine mullet are at times taken with tackle the reverse of fine. The method at this place is to fix up a paternoster of anything up to five or six hooks at intervals along its length, a heavy lead at the bottom and a " Fishing Gazette " float of good size. The fishing is done from the banks and the heavy weight is necessary in order to get the tackle out into the middle of the pools where the fish congregate. The bait is always ragworm and the fish are sometimes so plentiful and feeding so freely that two, or even occasionally three, may be taken at a time. It must be admitted, however, that these good feeding periods cannot be counted on and often, though the fish are plentiful in the pools, only a very occasional mullet can be tempted to take the bait.

A very much more sporting method of taking mullet is by the use of roach tackle. This, though, would not be of much use in the place I have just mentioned, as the banks are so high and muddy that all the fish have to be lifted out. Ordinary roach tackle would not be strong enough.

In some places mullet are taken on freshly baked bread. The tackle consists of a nine-foot trace of good gut with a weight of about half an ounce placed three or four feet above the bait. No float is used and if there is much wind another weight is placed on the line just above the gut to steady the tip of the rod. A small piece of the inside of the loaf is placed on the hook. The ideal is to have the bait hanging straight below the tip of the rod so that the bite is shown at once. The place should be ground-baited with stale bread soaked in sea-water until a bite indicates that the fish have come around; after that hard pellets should be thrown in occasionally, squeezed up so that they sink immediately. It is delicate fishing as the bite is shown by a very slight movement of the rod top. The strike must be immediate and the hooked fish played firmly, but with great care, since the mullet has a very soft mouth. At Portland the local men use this method, but watch the bait and strike when they see the mullet take it. It is essential that the hands should be perfectly clean when fishing by this method and using this bait and, if there is oil on the surface, ground-bait should be thrown in and the hook bait lowered through the hole thus made in the surface film.

Bread may also be used in surface-fishing for mullet. For this method a light rod should be used—a trout rod is excellent—and a fine line which must be dressed and well greased so that it will float. The tackle consists of about six feet of 2X gut and a No. 8 or No. 9 hook. Three or four small pieces of cork should be threaded on to the gut, the end one about six or eight inches from the hook, the others placed evenly along the gut cast; the corks should be pegged so that they will remain in place. If further weight is needed for casting, one of the corks may be larger than the others and should carry some lead. This weighted cork should not be pegged, but should be placed between two of the others. The mullet will not feel it if it exercises no check on the trace. The fish should be collected by throwing in a handful of bread-cubes and the bait should be a piece of new bread pinched on to the hook, brown bread being better than white.

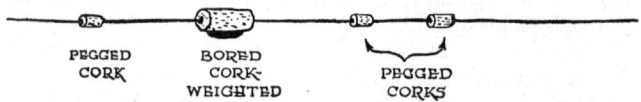

FLOATING MULLET TACKLE

Mullet may often be seen feeding on the maggots washed out of rotting seaweed as the tide rises over the rocks. If the floating tackle, already described for use with bread, is used and baited with a couple of maggots some good mullet may be captured.

Small strips of fresh herring are also good as bait for mullet, as are sections of boiled macaroni.

The Channel Islanders catch mullet on the stripped tail of a shrimp on a stout Limerick hook. They use a long rod and strong line and heave the fish out at once when hooked because a fighting fish will scare the others. They ground-bait by using boiled young prawns, shrimps, etc., which they catch in very fine nets and cook with salt. From time to time they place a small lump of this bait on the rocks and allow the tide to wash it off; the mullet soon find it and congregate round the spot.

It is always a good plan to ground-bait for sea-fish and various baits can be used for the purpose. Chopped worms, crushed crabs, mashed-up pilchards, mackerel or fresh herrings, etc., mixed with bread and bran make a very good ground-bait.

Conger and dogfish may be taken from the rocks, fishing in the gullies as the tide rises and letting the bait rest on the bottom. The bait may be any of the usual; but a very excellent one is a piece of bloater or kipper. As these baits are often preferred when rather " high ", it is a good plan to

SEA FISHING

save all heads, skins and tails from the breakfast-table for use within the next day or two as bait.

Bad luck with lead weights may run into rather a heavy expense. A good substitute is stones. It is not necessary to carry the stones with one, all that one need carry is some pieces of old rag and some string. To make this " Farewell "

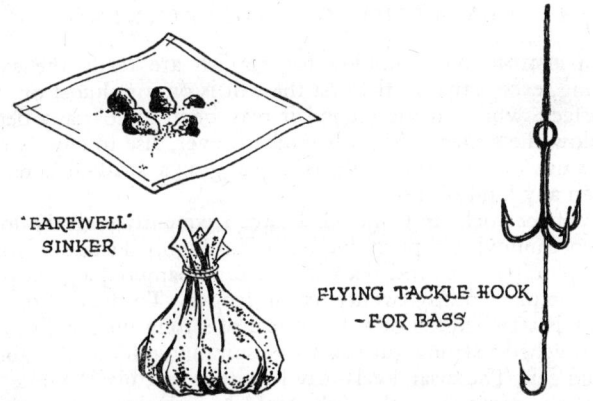

'FAREWELL' SINKER

FLYING TACKLE HOOK – FOR BASS

weight, fill a piece of rag with stones, tie it up with string and attach it by a piece of fine string to the end of the cast.

When bass are biting shyly and cannot be hooked it is a good plan to attach a single hook to the triangle on which the bait is carried so that it hangs about two inches below the bait. It will be found that it is on this flying hook that the fish will be taken.

Chapter X

SEA FISHING

FLY-FISHING AND SPINNING

FLY-FISHING and spinning for sea-fish are really the same thing, except that in the first the bait is on, or almost on, the surface, whilst in the second it may be at almost any depth below the surface. Sea-fish rarely, if ever, rise to any fly and the use of an artificial fly is to suggest a small fish rather than any kind of insect.

Off the rocks in Cornwall I have frequently seen the local men employing a primitive but often highly successful form of spinning. The rod is a whole natural bamboo, a great pole in one piece nearly twenty feet in length. To the end of this pole is attached ten or a dozen feet of strong line, and to this is attached a strong gut substitute spinning trace and a rubber sand-eel. These sand-eels may be either red, black, white, or green; sometimes the fish prefer one colour, sometimes another. The angler stands on the rocks as close to the waves as possible and swings his bait out into the foam, drawing it through the water past him to the full extent of the sweep of the rod. When a fish is hooked, it is played into an oncoming wave, coaxed well up on to the rocks and grabbed before it can be swept back again. The commonest fish to be caught by this method is the pollack; but bass also are sometimes taken.

The same method of fishing with a moving bait in the foam may be employed with spinning tackle and a running line, and baits may be either rubber sand-eels, phantoms, spinners, spinners with sole-skin baits attached, or artificial ragworms. The spinner, or rubber bait, is rarely heavy enough to enable one to cast any distance and a "Jardine" grooved weight, or some other form of weight must be attached to the trace. A useful artificial sand-eel for this style of fishing can be made from half the rubber-band, which lies

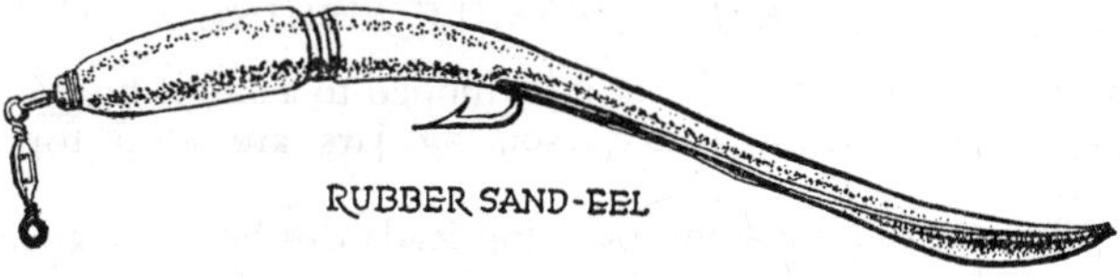

RUBBER SAND-EEL

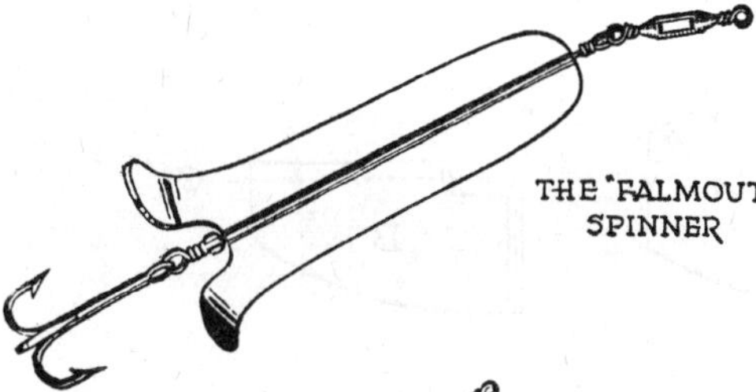

THE "FALMOUTH" SPINNER

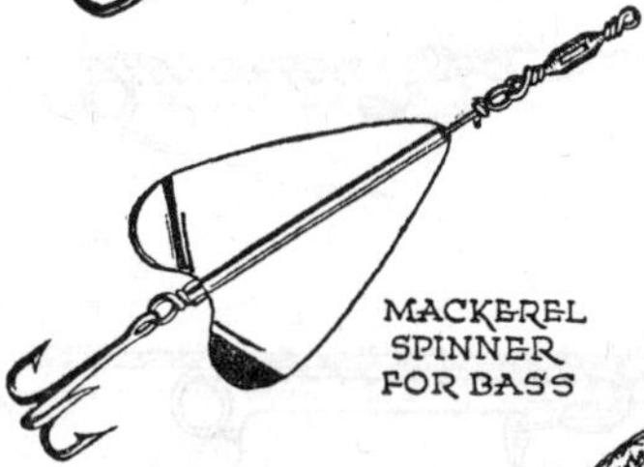

MACKEREL SPINNER FOR BASS

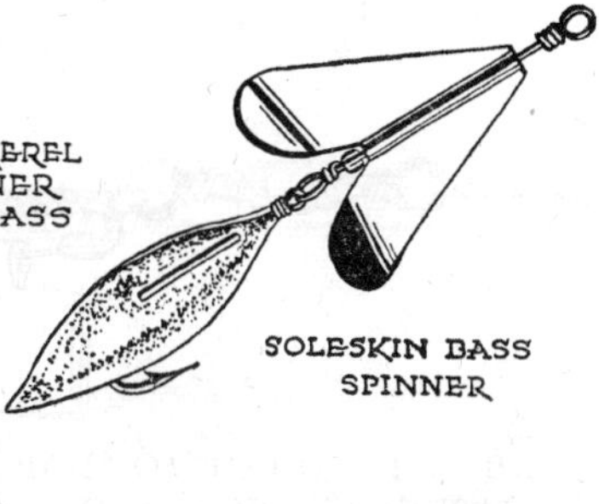

SOLESKIN BASS SPINNER

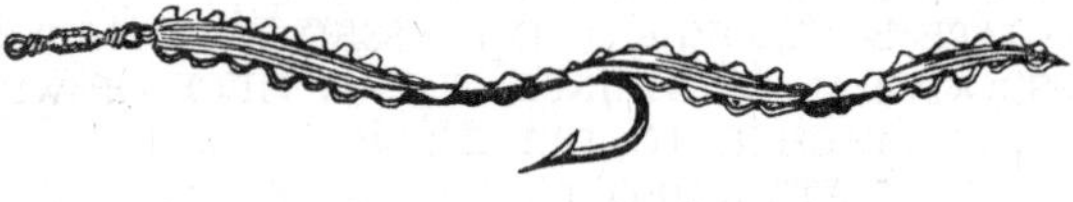

ARTIFICIAL LUG-WORM

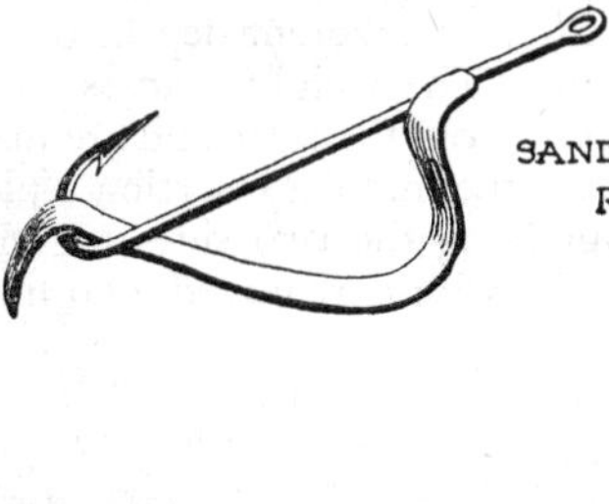

SAND-EEL MADE FROM RUBBER BAND

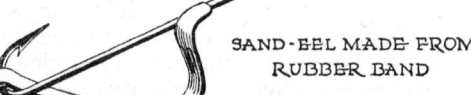

round the stopper of a big jar whipped to a single hook. The used bands from fruit-preserving jars are ideal for this purpose.

Satisfactory anti-kink spinning leads can be made at home from sheet lead and ordinary safety-pins. The back of the

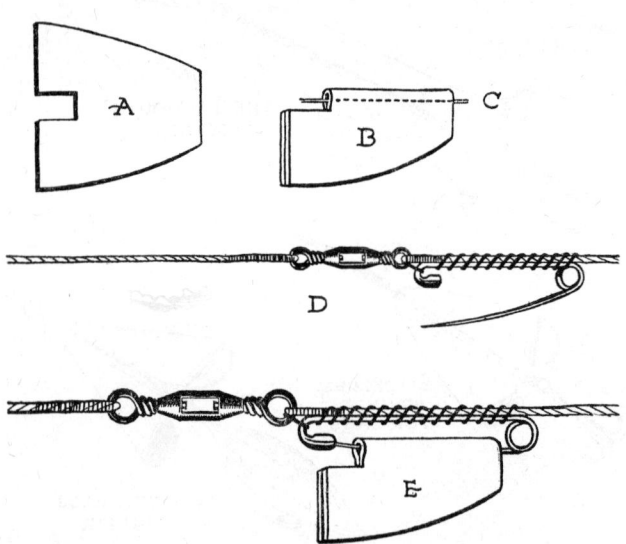

A—SHEET LEAD CUT TO SHAPE
B—SHAPE BENT OVER AND PRESSED TOGETHER
C—GROOVE MADE BY INSERTING A PIECE OF WIRE
D—PIN ATTACHED TO TRACE
E—WEIGHT ATTACHED TO PIN

safety-pin is wired to the spinning trace above the centre swivel. The leads can be cut with different depths of keel so as to be of different weights. The weights can be changed without taking the safety-pins from the trace and are made by folding the lead shapes down the middle, inserting a piece of wire, and hammering or pressing the two sides together so that a groove is left when the wire is removed. To fix: the

SEA FISHING

safety-pin is unfastened, the lead slipped on to the pin, and the pin then closed.

The line used for spinning should be as fine as is consistent with strength, bearing in mind that one may often have to fight with strong fish of five or six pounds weight. Naturally it is much easier to cast with a fine light line than with a thick heavy one.

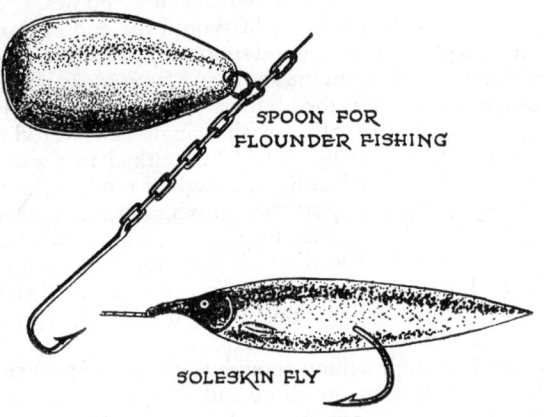

SPOON FOR FLOUNDER FISHING

SOLESKIN FLY

One may spin from the shore, from the rocks, or from a boat. Good sport may also be had spinning in estuaries. Flounders will often take a spinning spoon bait, provided it is baited with a ragworm, lugworm, or strip of mackerel. The spoon used for this style of fishing is specially fitted with a hook trailing well clear of the spoon itself, and this hook is baited with the ragworm, or other bait. The hook and bait must not spin, so it is necessary to have at least one swivel between it and the spoon. This baited spinner is fished slowly close to the bottom. The flounder apparently wakes up on seeing the spoon and this enables it to spot the bait trailing behind it.

Fly-fishing for sea-fish is already very popular in many places, the famous Filey Brig stands often being almost uncomfortably full of anglers; but the extraordinary variety of fish which have been taken by this sporting method of angling suggests that it might be employed with success much more frequently than it is. Coal-fish, pollack, bass, mackerel are all taken fairly regularly with the fly—it would seem that any fish willing to take " brit " on the surface might be taken at the right time by fly.

The usual sea fly may be either a white feather or a strip of white sole-skin attached to a hook, and very little else. The more elaborate flies often have red and silver bodies.

The season for bass is from May until the end of August, and throughout this period good sport may be had in estuaries and in certain places from the shore and from rocks with a fly. A two-handed fly-rod is the ideal weapon, because with it one can cast so much farther than with a single-handed rod; but either will serve. The fly should be worked in short jerks and, though the fish taken by this method rarely exceed two pounds in weight, the sport they provide on the light tackle used more than compensates for their individual lack of size. When bass are found feeding close to the surface no time should be lost in getting to work on them. The " rise " is usually of short duration. But, while it lasts, the sport will probably be fast and furious.

Mackerel, though willing enough to take the fly when they can be found close to the shore and feeding on the surface, unfortunately do not give one many opportunities.

Pollack up to a pound in weight may sometimes be taken on the fly in harbours, after dark, fishing in the beams of the harbour lamps. They may also be taken off the shore over shallow weed beds, particularly towards sunset.

The link between bait-fishing and fly-fishing is clearly shown in a method employed at Scarborough. As many as seven or eight plain white flies made from duck's feathers are strung along a cast at intervals of six to eight inches. A light lead is fastened to the head of the cast and another smaller lead to the other end. The tackle is then lowered into the water and jerked up and down in a manner much like the sink-and-draw method of fishing a dead minnow for trout. Great catches of coal-fish are often made in this way. Cod, mackerel and occasionally other fish are also caught.

Fly-fishing or spinning for sea-fish may be done either from the shore or from a boat. In most cases larger fish are

SEA FISHING

taken when a boat is employed. In almost every case one fishes in shallow water over shoals and sandbanks or in estuaries or inlets. The west coasts of both Scotland and Ireland provide good spots; so also are there many good spots along the coast of Wales. Good bass fishing is to be had off the Isle of Wight and in many places on the coasts of

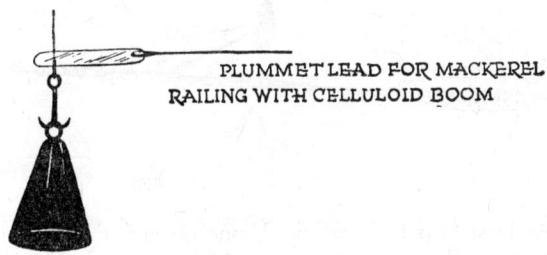

PLUMMET LEAD FOR MACKEREL RAILING WITH CELLULOID BOOM

Devon and Cornwall. The Eddystone Lighthouse is one of the best places for bass fishing—when the sea is sufficiently placid at this somewhat rough spot to allow one to fish.

Mackerel-railing, as it is usually conducted, can hardly be called angling, since a hand-line only is used and the fish hauled in with little or no playing. The tackle consists of a heavy lead, up to two pounds in weight, and shaped like a plummet. The reason for using this type of lead is that when one is fishing from a boat, either being sailed or rowed over the fishing ground, this flat-bottomed lead will stand steadily on deck when hauled in instead of rolling about as a round lead would do. Above the lead is fixed a short celluloid boom and to this is attached about two fathoms of cotton snooding, followed by a gut collar a yard long, complete with swivel and spinner. If a fresh mackerel can be obtained the spinner is baited with a " sneed ", or " last ", cut from the tail of the fish. This " sneed " is a silvery strip of flesh about two to three inches long. To bait the hook, the " sneed " is laid, silvery side downwards, on a piece of cork and the hook driven through it until it penetrates the cork. When the hook is withdrawn from the cork, the " sneed " will be in position in the bend. If a mackerel is not available, a piece of white kid glove, a white feather, or a slip of silver paper will do almost as well; and, if a spinner is not at hand, a plain hook with a "sneed" of some sort on it will often answer.

When railing, the boat is sailed, or rowed, at about five miles an hour and the tackle let out on about five fathoms of

SPINNER

line. At least two lines are used, one on either side of the boat, and, if there are more than two persons in the boat other lines may be employed on outriggers (poles or spare oars put out at right-angles over the sides of the boat). As soon as a shoal of fish is found, the boat is kept moving backwards and forwards over the spot. The fish are hauled in hand-over-hand and care must be taken to see that they are lifted in clear of the side of the boat as it is very easy to knock them from the hook. The best catches are usually made during the early morning or evening. But quite frequently good catches are made in the middle of the day.

Mackerel have no particular haunts. They move about freely from place to place and may be found sometimes so close to the shore that they may be dipped out, at other times well out to sea. When the mackerel are "in", the boats go out and sail until they strike a shoal. The chief skill then rests rather with the management of the boat than with the angler; for the boat must be kept moving at a suitable pace, neither too fast nor too slowly, and must not lose contact with the fish.

Chapter XI

SEA FISHING

BOAT-FISHING

Though one may fish with a fly or a spinner from a boat, and much of the best of both these types of fishing is to be had when afloat, the subject of boat-fishing may well be dealt with under a separate heading, because it is only from a boat that one of the most interesting methods of taking sea-fish can usually be followed. I refer to drift-line fishing with a fly-rod. The method is as follows:

Use for preference a split-cane fly-rod fitted with a suitable reel and at least fifty yards of silk line well dressed with animal fat and terminating in a lake trout gut, or gut substitute, cast fitted with a swivel and a long-shanked hook. If the tide is not too strong no weight other than the swivel is necessary. The depth is first plumbed and the line marked by passing a small piece of worsted, or coloured silk, through it with a needle, tying the silk or worsted round the line and cutting off the ends. The hook is then baited with a "last" of mackerel, a live prawn, or a live sand-eel, and paid out until the spot marked is at the surface of the water. The bait will now be about six feet from the bottom. If the tide strengthens, pay out more line. The bait is moved with a slow sink-and-draw action and, when the bait is a prawn, unless the bite is in the nature of a decided "run", striking should not follow too quickly on the first touch as it is essential that the prawn should be well within the fish's mouth to ensure hooking.

It is, of course, necessary to have a landing net for any form of light rod-fishing from a boat. Though one may beach quite large fish when using a trout rod from a shelving shore, it is next to impossible to lift even a relatively small one into a boat—certainly not without risking considerable damage to the rod.

It is by drift-line fishing that one may take that most sporting fish, the black bream. Unfortunately, these fish are to be found in a few localities only. The Sussex coast is the place most favoured; but they are available for only a short period during the spring and early summer. The best time of the day is the early morning and the bait should be fished as close to the bottom as one can without fouling the rocks and weed.

Ground-baiting is almost a necessity in black bream fishing and the favourite ground-bait is pounded spider crab. But, if this is not to be had, mussels and other shell-fish will do almost as well.

Black bream fishing has been carried on so intensively at some stations, particularly at Bognor, that the fish have become almost as shy as the best educated roach—which seems to suggest that the same fish return each year to the same spots for spawning. When the bream are biting shyly, it is often a good plan not to be in too much hurry to strike, but to pay out a little more line at the first suggestion of a nibble in order to encourage the fish to take hold more boldly.

When the tide has steadied to such an extent that the line is no longer carried away from the boat it is time to stop drift-lining and put on float-tackle.

The red bream is another fish, not quite so vigorous in its fighting as the black bream, which may also be taken by the drift-line method. This fish is found chiefly on the south-western coasts and the best time of the day to fish for it is evening. Bait may be either lugworm, ragworm, mackerel or herring and, whereas it is often unsafe to use more than one hook when fishing for the more active black bream, it is usually fairly safe to use two hooks for the red variety.

The depth must be plumbed when fishing for red bream and it may be as well to remark here that it is a good plan to mark the line with different coloured threads of silk for the different depths—every five fathoms is a useful division.

Unfortunately, in many places where red bream are to be found the tides run too strongly for the use of very light tackle. The only thing to do in these circumstances is to fish with a stouter rod, a relatively heavier lead and in paternoster

SEA FISHING

style with two or three hooks. The season for these fish is from about the beginning of June to the end of September.

Some anglers when bream fishing use fine wire mountings to their hooks as a protection against dogfish, which are frequently found in the same localities. When drift-line fishing with a very light rod it may be just as well to let the dogfish carry off the hook as to risk spoiling the rod by having to fight one of these lugging brutes on it. Pollack also have a habit of turning up at these times and they, too, will generally get the better of the argument when they make their well-known dive into the depths of the weeds. But, since the red bream is not really a very valiant fighter, it is perhaps preferable to fish for him with light tackle and risk an occasional break with something larger.

Almost every kind of sea-fish may be taken by the drift-line method of fishing provided the depth is not more than ten fathoms. The tackle used must, of course, be heavier when one is after some of the larger kinds, and the rod should be something more in the nature of a pike rod. The usual pike rod, reel and line will answer perfectly for any of the relatively large sea-fish likely to be found in the bays and a short distance off shore anywhere round the British Isles. If one is fishing with a float it will almost always be necessary to use a slider and a stop formed by tying a small piece of rubber-band to the line at the depth required.

Hooks used for sea-fishing are often much too large. If one is using the lighter styles already recommended, size 10 is quite large enough for almost any ordinary fish. A large hook requires a strong and heavy rod to drive it home; when using a light rod and a large hook, one will miss a large number of fish by failure to get the hook into their mouths over the barb.

Railing for mackerel with a hand-line has already been dealt with; but this fish may also be taken by a somewhat similar method but with a trout rod. If the mackerel are on the small side two hooks can be used and these should be baited with a " last " cut from a dead mackerel into the form of a small fish. A pair of nail scissors should be used to cut the shape in the skin and a very sharp knife used to pare it from the body. This imitation fish is hooked through the part where its eye might be supposed to be and trailed behind a moving boat. Dead white-bait serve the same purpose very well; they should be hooked through the eyes. When a mackerel is hooked on one bait, it is a good plan to let it play for a few moments. This will cause the other bait to dart about and it also will soon be taken by a second mackerel.

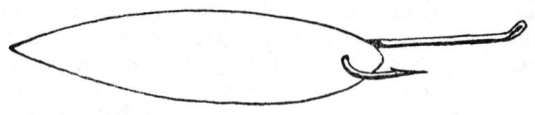

MACKEREL SKIN BAIT
(ACTUAL SIZE)

But, if the mackerel are large, only one hook should be used as this fish is such a fierce fighter that two large ones at once will be too much for the rod. The same type of tackle and bait may also be used from a drifting boat and worked sink and draw. If a garfish takes the bait, as it is likely to do if there is one about, the angler will have no cause for complaint about any dullness in the fishing.

The best time of the day for this style of fishing is early in the morning and during the evening. It is not a method favoured by the professional, who usually counts the success of an outing solely by the number of fish taken. It is, therefore, better to go with an angling companion of a similar turn of mind to oneself, one who will thoroughly enjoy taking a dozen fish in a really sporting manner; whereas the professional would consider this a waste of time when he could have returned with four times that number in the boat by using the hand-line method of railing. I have found that this holds good with much sea-fishing and, except for the purpose of finding marks in strange waters, always prefer to go with an angling friend without the assistance of the professional.

The hake is a fine fighting fish, but does not figure very often in the sea-angler's catch, because it is mainly a night feeder. The simplest way of arranging a hake fishing outing is to arrange to go out with the mackerel, herring or pilchard drifters, and spend the night on board. The tackle should be

SEA FISHING

a wire trace, six or eight feet in length, and the hook about size 10/0. The best bait is a fresh herring or mackerel hooked just behind the head. The professional fisherman always use a very long-shanked hook when fishing for hake because of the formidable teeth this fish has. But perhaps the simplest method for the rod-angler is to use normally shanked hooks and attach them to the trace by a spring link swivel. If before setting out the angler provides himself with half a dozen hooks attached to foot-long pieces of piano wire, each with a loop at the end, the hook and fish can be detached together from the trace and a new hook mounted. This is much easier than struggling with the hook by the light of a ship's lantern. Fishing cannot start until the nets are down and then the first thing to do is to find the depth. The weight, which need not be more than a couple of ounces, is attached to the end of the line and lowered into the water until it is felt to strike the bottom. The line is then reeled in for about three fathoms and marked with a piece of white wool. Then mount the wire trace below the weight, attach the baited hook to the spring link at the end, and lower until the mark in the line appears. The bait should be fished sink and draw. When the bite is felt (and the bite of a hake is pretty vigorous), do not strike at once, but let the fish have a second or two to get it well into its mouth. A warm, quiet night is usually the best.

The cod is taken usually during the autumn months and the favourite bait in England is the lugworm. In Ireland and Scotland mackerel or herring is generally used. When it is found that a shoal of cod have been encountered the angler must take care not to strike too soon and, when he has hooked a fish, to play it delicately as these fish are often only lightly hooked. Tackle similar to that used in pollack fishing may be employed; but where heavy fish may be expected, such as on the west coasts of Ireland and Scotland, it is as well to use wire in place of gut substitute for the trace.

The whiting is a popular fish with hand-liners; but, since it is rarely met with above a pound in weight, it is not so much in favour with rod-anglers. Whiting feed near the sea bed, usually over a sandy bottom and, when a shoal is struck, one may be pretty sure of getting a large number of fish. The season varies. Along the south coast the earlier summer months are often the best, but on the east coast these fish are more usually encountered during the autumn. Paternoster tackle is as good as any; but, if the fish seem at all shy, it is often a good plan to have one hook on a short trace hanging below the lead. The hooks must be fairly small and the bait may be almost any of the usual sea-baits. In the latter part of the autumn portions of sprat are frequently the best bait on the south-east coast.

The pouting is another popular fish with boating parties using hand-lines. In English waters it does not run large; but what it lacks in size it more than makes up for in numbers. It is commonly found over sunken reefs and has an unfortunate liking for the neighbourhood of wrecks, so that losses of tackle may be frequent. A pound fish may be considered large for English waters. On the west coast of Ireland, however, they are at times found above three pounds in weight. Pouting feed close to the bottom. A paternoster, with one hook attached below the lead, makes satisfactory tackle. For bait one may use almost anything—small pieces of herring, pilchard, mackerel, mussels, lugworm, ragworm, or soft crab. Pouting fishing can be a very pleasant amusement on a warm day and in a calm sea. If bait should run out owing to there being many fish at the spot, pieces cut from a dead pouting will often capture others.

The last of the lesser sporting fish of our seas is the wrasse. This is a rock-haunting fish, often found close inshore and sometimes running to several pounds in weight. It will take almost any bait and, so far as my own experience goes, is the only fish that will take limpet. The flesh is rather soft and it is not usually considered worth using as human food, though I have often eaten and enjoyed wrasse baked in milk. It is, however, usually welcomed as bait by the crab and lobster fishermen. Perhaps its chief interest to the observant angler lies in the beauty and variety of its colouring. Wrasse feed close to the bottom and, whereas a single-hooked paternoster is good, tackle with the hook below the weight will often do better if one can be sure of not becoming hung up in rocks or weed every time it is put out. Wrasse take some time to get the bait into their mouths. It is, therefore, necessary to wait a little while after the first nibble. When the fish is hooked it at once dives for the holes in the rocks, and its initial pull is usually very powerful. It is advisable to use a wire trace and wire snooding as the fish has very strong teeth and has a habit of getting under overhanging ledges of rocks and thereby cutting a gut substitute trace. Perhaps the most interesting way of taking wrasse is to fish for them in clear water on a calm day and to fish by sight, striking when one sees that the fish has taken the bait. They may be taken throughout the summer and right on till the end of November. The best time to fish is during the first two hours after dead low water.

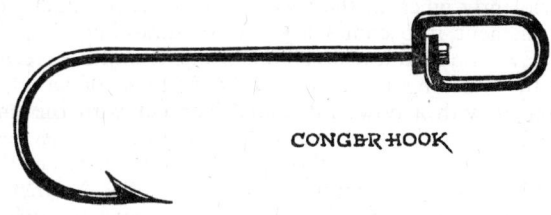

CONGER HOOK

Whether fishing for conger may be considered sport is largely a matter of point of view. The conger does not run and the management of it on the line devolves into straight pulling. Many more conger are caught by night than by day and it is usually at night that the larger specimens are taken. Since this fish does not run there is little to be gained by the use of a rod; in fact, it is better not to use a rod if one is at all likely to meet with heavy specimens. Hooks for conger should have swivelled eyes and there should be several swivels on the trace. Some people recommend that the trace should be of wire; others state that the conger objects to anything of a hard or stiff nature near the bait. Whatever is used must be very strong—the pull of a ten-pound conger may well be taken for that of a fish at least five times as heavy. Conger often play about with the bait for a long while before getting it into their mouths, and it is sometimes necessary to wait nearly a quarter of an hour before driving the hook home. As soon as the fish is hooked it will at once attempt to get down under or round the rocks and this must be prevented at all costs. A steady pull must be kept up the whole time.

But, if the conger does get a grip on a rock with its tail it will generally let go if the pull is slackened for a few moments. It is not safe to use more than one hook in conger-fishing, and this must be baited with a good lump of quite fresh bait. Young octopus is probably the best, but is often difficult to procure. Squid is almost as good; but this also is not always at hand. Herring, pilchard or mackerel are all good baits and nine out of ten conger caught by hook and line are probably taken on one or other of these. The most exciting part of conger fishing is when the fish is in the boat. Though it merely lugs hard, turns round and round, and shakes its head violently when in the water, as soon as it is taken out of its element it becomes a twisting, thrashing, snapping fiend. Even on land it takes all one's time to still the creature either by knocking it out with a heavy billet of wood, or stabbing it with a powerful knife. The cut with the knife should be at the back of the head so as to sever the spinal column. Some people hit the conger on the tail rather than the head when stunning it with a piece of wood. Neither the head nor the tail is particularly easy to hit; but I am inclined to think that a really good whack on the tail puts the fish out more quickly than when hit on the head.

Chapter XII

SEA FISHING

BIG GAME

THE fish dealt with under this heading are not usually fished for by the ordinary sea-angler. In most cases a special equipment, including special rod and reel, is required, and, although in some cases this can be hired, an outing after one of the " big game " fish of British waters may be a rather expensive business.

I am including in this section skate, ling, shark, tope and tunny.

Skate are to be found pretty generally round the British Isles; but the largest are probably around the coasts of Scotland, Western Ireland and Cornwall. Very few anglers go fishing for skate; such as they do catch are usually caught by chance. Most anglers who have caught one, perhaps weighing something in the neighbourhood of a hundredweight, consider the one experience enough for a lifetime. In all probability the angler starts with the intention of managing it himself; but after spending a considerable time, apparently lifting up the bottom of the sea, he usually accepts the help of the boatman and sees his catch eventually brought within reach of the gaff by being hand-lined to the surface. With a large skate the tug-of-war, which constitutes the sporting side of the adventure, may last upwards of an hour, most of which time will be occupied in getting the fish off the bottom and keeping it from getting down again. The bait is usually a whole mackerel, herring or pilchard fished on the bottom.

The ling is found chiefly off the Scottish and Irish coasts, and also off Cornwall, particularly from Land's End to the Scillies. It feeds fairly close to the bottom and may be taken on herring, pilchard, mackerel or portions of almost any other fish. The trace should be of wire and the hook fished below the weight. The bite is often rather prolonged and it therefore pays to give the fish plenty of time. The best time of the year is usually from January until the end of May.

Sharks are found around the coasts of Devon, Cornwall and Western Ireland, chiefly during the hottest months of the year and when the sea is calm. At such times the sharks (chiefly blue sharks) swim high in the water and may be seen with their triangular back fins sticking out as they slowly cruise about.

The trace for shark fishing must be of steel and fitted with plenty of swivels; the hook also should be of the swivel-eyed type and size suggested for conger. A float is commonly used, similar to that used for pike fishing, and there should be several free-running pilot floats above the main float to prevent the line sinking and getting round the trace. Since the fishing is often a sort of side-line to pollack, or other, fishing, the bait can well be the heads and remains of mackerel, herring and such-like as have been used as bait for the smaller fish. It is not necessary to cast a long way from the boat as sharks have little fear and will take the bait within a few yards of an anchored boat. The bite of a shark is usually unmistakable, the float going down and away with a bang. If the rod is put down whilst waiting for the shark to lay hold, the end should be no more than a couple of feet over the side of the boat. When it is intended that a part at any rate of the day's outing shall be spent in shark fishing, a float should be provided for the moorings and the painter released as soon as the shark is hooked. The bait should be as large as the hook will carry.

The tope is met with chiefly in the Thames Estuary during the summer. It feeds on the bottom and is often taken in quite shallow water. The bait may be almost any salt-water fish, whiting or pouting being favourites, though mackerel or herring may do equally well. The tope takes the bait in a manner very different from the shark, often picking it up and dropping it again several times before it finally decides to swallow it. When a tope runs off with the bait, no attempt should be made to stop it until it has gone forty or fifty yards; it should then be struck very hard, for it has a very tough mouth and only very sharp hooks driven with considerable power behind them will effect an entrance and make

SEA FISHING

a hold. The trace should be of wire and should be well furnished with swivels. The weight should be of the ledger type with holes, or rings, sufficiently large to allow the line to run quite freely.

The fact that tunny have been taken in fair numbers off the coast of Brittany and off the Yorkshire coast suggests that other stations where this splendid fish may be caught within reach of the English coast will be found. The other " big game " already referred to can be and often are (by accident usually) taken on ordinary strong sea-rods and tackle ; but the tunny quite definitely requires a special outfit and therefore cannot be dealt with under ordinary sea-fishing. It also requires a special purse !

PART IV

TROUT, SALMON AND
SEA-TROUT FISHING

Chapter XIII

FLY-FISHING

GENERAL

EVENTUALLY the angler, whatever his experience, whatever his usual practice, will try his hand at fly-fishing. And from the moment that he sees his line sailing out in that most beautiful of curves, to land lightly on the water, straight and accurately placed, feels the poetry of the movement of a good rod in his hands, experiences the sight of a head and tail rise or the solid tug of a fish well hooked, he is lost—lost for ever to the charms of the most glorious, thrilling and satisfying art that is vouched to the brotherhood of fishermen.

Fly-fishing is not, as is so often imagined, the prerogative of the rich. Fly-fishing, in one form or another is within the reach and pocket of every angler in Britain. Though perhaps one of the lucky ones myself in the possession of a first-class salmon beat, nevertheless some of the best salmon fishing I have ever enjoyed has been absolutely free. I remember, too, as red letter days, fishing for sea-trout in the sea itself off our northern islands, with great big flies while wading amongst the rafts of seaweed. I remember happy hours spent in tempting grayling in November in northern streams with the finest of tackle and tiny flies; catching silvery dace in the sluggish streams of Essex and Suffolk, drifting half the length of Coniston and Windermere Lakes and catching beautiful golden trout in the April breeze, wading in the brackish water of many estuaries and taking sea-trout of all sizes, and even on one never-to-be-forgotten occasion, an eighteen-pound salmon! These are the great occasions of fishing, and just as for the true lover of shooting it is the hours spent on the saltings rewarded by an occasional shot at duck or geese—shooting that is free to every man—that lives in the memory long after the holocausts of 500 pheasants or 200 brace of grouse have been forgotten, so are these days, the wild and untrammelled days of fishing, remembered when the big days on strictly preserved waters are forgotten. If you can afford a fly-rod and line, then you can not only afford fly-fishing, but you can enjoy the best of it.

Fly-fishing requires certain special tackle and demands a certain technique in using it. To be able to cast a fly properly is a *sine qua non*, and while no amount of written instruction can take the place of practice and tuition on the water, nevertheless, much can be achieved if the neophyte will take the trouble to understand the theory of casting and will practise on any lawn before going down to the water.

The whole " reason " for casting is that you shall be able to present a lure to the fish at such a distance from you that, in the clear waters where this form of fishing is practised, you do not frighten him either by your proximity or by splashing the line into the water.

How is this achieved? Let us for the moment suppose that you have acquired a ten-foot trout rod and a properly balanced tapered line. You now go out on to a lawn, put up your rod and line and start off.

The object, we have said, is to throw your line, *straight*, away from you in a given direction. The first thing to remember is that it is not your arm itself that will effect this, but the instrument which you hold in your hand. It is the rod which casts the line, and it does so by virtue of the energy which you impart to it by the movement of your arm. You are doing now what every games player that uses a bat, a stick or a racket does. A golfer imparts a certain movement to the head of the club which hits the ball. It is the club that the golfer controls, not the ball. So, too, the cricketer, the hockey or tennis player. So, too, the fly fisherman.

The problem, then, resolves itself into determining how to make the rod pick up and throw the line, rather than how to do it oneself. And it is because so many people fail to realise this that fly-casting is often so very poorly mastered.

Let us look at it another way. Why do we have to use a rod at all? Why cannot we pick up the line in our hands and cast it with our arm? The answer is one purely of dynamics. Twenty yards of line weighs no more than an ounce or two. But it has a large surface. Consequently it requires to be moved very fast through the air to overcome air resistance.

TROUT, SALMON AND SEA-TROUT FISHING

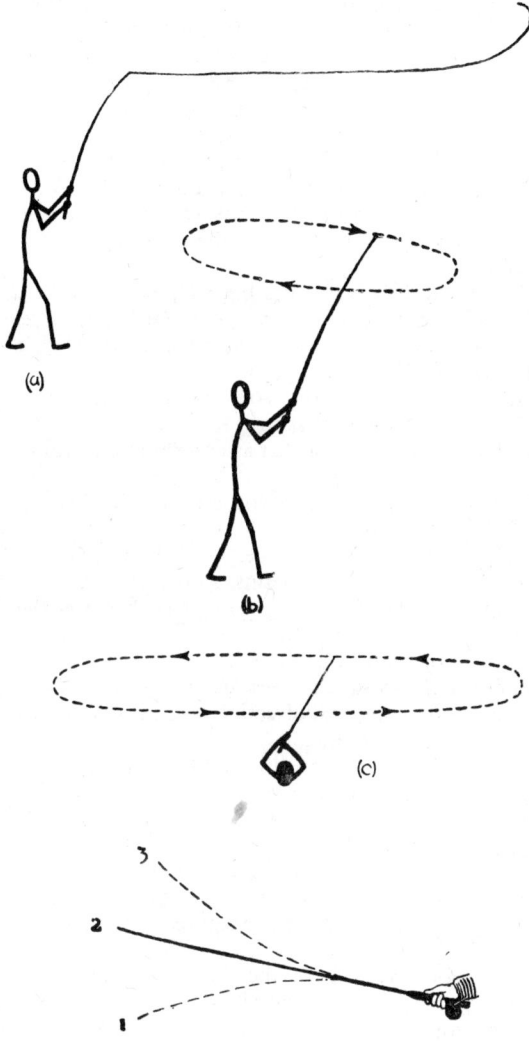

Your arm, though having plenty of power, cannot move *fast* enough to throw the line. Therefore, you utilise the lever principle, in reverse as it were, in order to turn the excess power in your arm into speed. This is what David did when he put the stone into a sling and killed Goliath. He lengthened, in effect, his arm and gave the stone more speed and more energy.

The object of the rod, then, is primarily to make the line move faster. And since the line is virtually attached to the rod point, it is this portion of it which requires to be moved at speed.

Now the whippiness in a casting rod, just as in the shaft of a golf club, is there for one purpose only: to increase the speed at which the point of the rod travels through a given arc. If you hold the rod in your hand parallel to the ground and lift it sharply upwards you will notice, if you watch carefully, that when you first start to move the butt, the point still stays where it was, but that after a short interval it begins to move and soon, not only catches up with the butt, but actually passes it immediately you cease to lift. The diagram shows this quite clearly.

It is this power of moving the tip of the rod very fast that is utilised by the angler in casting a line. And the first thing to bear in mind when learning to cast is that it is the tip of the rod which must be made to do all the work. To effect this, the butt of the rod is moved.

Casting the line now becomes merely an exercise in throwing a light body in a given direction when it is slung from the end of a long, whippy stick.

Forget, for the moment, all about the line, but imagine that you have a small stone stuck not very firmly on to the end ring of your rod. Lift your rod up to slightly beyond that vertical position over your shoulder and now make a movement as if to throw the imaginary stone as far forward—not downwards, but forwards—as you can. It is quite easy. And this is exactly the movement required to throw the line forward.

But first you have to lift the line up to a position from which it can be thrown forward. In other words you have got to get your imaginary stone attached to the end of the rod before you can throw it. Now since the line is long and thin there is only one position for it to be in if the movement of the tip of the rod can move it *all* at the same time: and this position is directly in a straight line away from the direction in which the rod is to be moved. So to throw the line forwards, we must first throw it back. And we do this in precisely the same manner as we throw our imaginary pebble forwards, but in a reverse direction and rather up in the air than directly level over our shoulder.

We do not want the line to fall to the ground behind us so we do our backward cast as if our pebble was to be thrown with an initial trajectory of about 45 degrees from the horizontal. And for this purpose we start our cast from rather below 30 degrees in front of us to slightly beyond the vertical, thus:

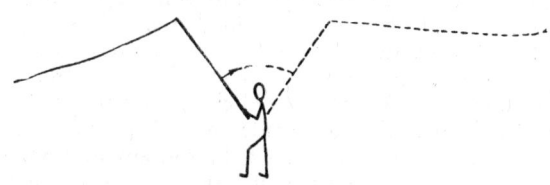

Having completed this backward throw, and remembering that we have to get the line out almost straight behind us before any movement of the rod tip can pull it all forward at once, it stands to reason that we must pause for a moment before making our forward throw in order to give the line time to straighten out.

Here, for most beginners, is where the difficulty lies. But the difficulty is, to my way of thinking, more because the beginner fails to realise that certain dynamical laws apply to the art of casting just as much as to the movement of a lift in a shaft. And one of the fundamental laws states that a body in motion will continue to travel in the same direction until something stops it. In this case the line, travelling backwards over your shoulder, will continue to travel in that direction until a " something "—the rod tip—prevents it continuing. And since it has a momentum it will exert a pull on the rod tip when the latter attempts to stop its motion.

In other words, if you throw the line back over your shoulder and wait, as soon as it straightens out it will give a pull on the rod tip and, if you are holding the rod steady and firm, will tend to flex it backwards.

This, obviously, is the moment when you must start your forward throw, and none other. It is virtually useless attempting to acquire the rhythm required to cast a line by any arbitrary rules as to the length of time you must wait after the back-cast before commencing your forward throw. This period will vary with the length of line you are throwing, the speed at which you throw it and with every gust of wind that opposes or assists its movement. There is only one moment when the forward throw should be started, and that is the moment when the line, by pulling on the rod tip, indicates that it is almost straight out behind you.

It will be realised that once the rod has reached the slightly more than vertical position required for the back throw it must on no account be moved either forwards or backwards until the forward cast is made. Why? Because we want to throw the line always as a whole, and any movement of the rod tip while the line is still travelling backwards will also move that part of the line which has already arrived in its proper position, and will, if persisted in, merely tend to arrest the backward movement of the remainder without throwing it forward.

In figures A to G opposite I have shown what happens to the rod and the hands at different phases of this crucial period of a cast.

A shows the hands pulling the rod back. The rod is flexed forward under the weight of the line on the tip.

B and C show the movement when the rod tip has imparted sufficient momentum to the line to lift it and start it at its greatest speed on its backward journey.

D shows the rod now straight with the line beginning to travel out behind. There is no pull on the rod and the hands are motionless.

E shows the line beginning now to exert a slight pull on the

TROUT, SALMON AND SEA-TROUT FISHING 127

rod tip since more of it is now being brought to a standstill than is still moving.

F shows the line almost straight out behind the rod and

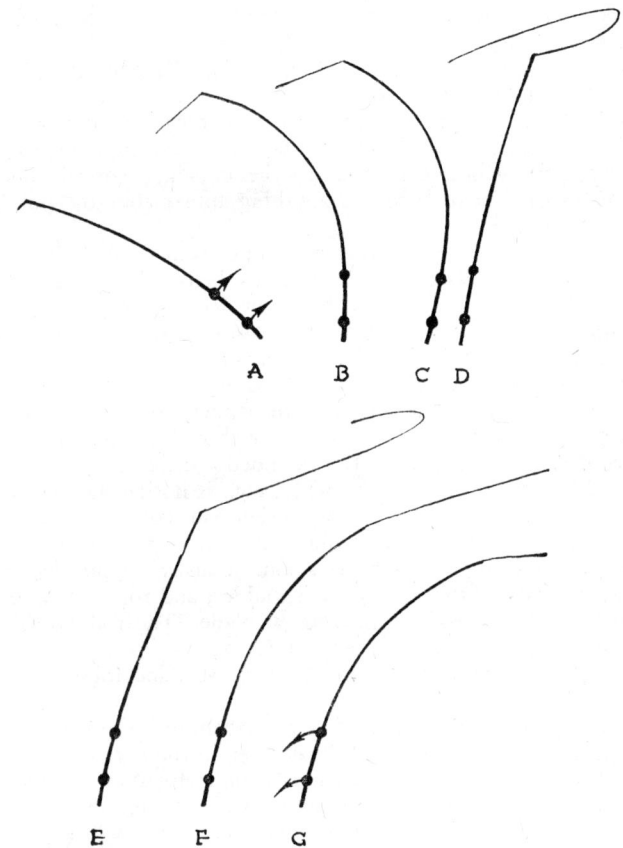

now exerting its maximum flexing energy on the steadily held rod.

G shows the hands now beginning to make the forward

cast and the rod flexing again under the movement of the butt which is not yet transmitted to the top joint and line.

Here, in theory, is how to make the perfect cast! And whereas without obeying these theoretical rules very nearly exactly it is impossible ever to cast well, certain factors exist which modify them slightly.

The first is the " fact " of air resistance. This has the effect of slowing up the movement of the last foot or two of the line, cast and fly, to such an extent that they have not, when allied to the fact that the ends of tapered lines, and casts, have very little weight compared to the remainder of the line, sufficient momentum to add anything appreciable to " pull " on the rod tip.

This means, in effect, that we do not wait until the line is entirely straightened out behind us before beginning the forward cast, but do so while a few feet still remain " uncurled ".

The second is the fact that we have got to make sure that, in uncurling, the fly does not catch up on the extended portion of the line. In theory this will not happen provided that the line is thrown backwards sufficiently above the horizontal to keep the fly always above the extended portion, see p. 123.

In practice this, owing to wind, etc., is not always easy to achieve. So practically every fisherman compromises by bringing the rod back in a different vertical plane to that in which he brings it forward again. Usually anglers throw backwards slightly outside the shoulder, and forwards more nearly with the rod in the vertical plane. The rod tip thus describes an elongated ellipse, see p. 123.

And, of course, the path taken by the line follows this curve, too, see p. 123.

The general mechanics of casting then, are no more than as described above. The difficulty lies in the correct timing of the forward throw. But it is a difficulty that is largely imaginary and which, if the angler will wait for the signal, precise and definite, which the line itself gives, will entirely disappear. No method of counting or artificial timing of the " waiting " period will do—nor can an onlooker by calling out " back—wait—forward " ever impart the required rhythm. Learn to recognise and feel the line's own signal and you can pick up any rod in the world and cast a decent line with it straight away.

It is well worth learning how to cast *before* choosing a rod to buy. Otherwise you will be at the mercy of the salesman who may know little more about the subject than you do yourself. Let us suppose that you have now mastered the rudiments of casting—the little tricks of shooting and mending, and so on, will come later—and you decide it is time to buy yourself a trout rod.

You are now faced with an important decision. What precisely do you expect of your rod? Are you going to fish exclusively for trout with a dry fly in chalk streams, or will your fly-fishing excursions take you to many different waters for many types of fish. How much, too, can you afford to spend on your tackle?

The fact of the matter is that whereas rods built specially for one type of fishing undoubtedly fulfil their purpose better than a general rod, yet the difference in the hands of a skilled fisherman is not really important, and it resolves itself finally into a question of comfort rather than utility. And I would suggest that for a start, at any rate, no attempt should be made to buy other than a fly-rod which can be used equally well for all except the heavier forms of salmon fishing.

There is a tendency nowadays to use increasingly shorter rods and lighter tackle. And I am not sure that this tendency has not been carried to extremes. But whereas an eight foot six inch rod with a very fine line may be a pleasure to fish with in one of the smaller chalk streams in summer, such a rod would be absolutely useless in Loch Harray in the Orkneys, for instance, when fishing from a boat in boisterous spring weather.

For a general-purpose rod that may be used for sea-trout, loch-trout, dace, grayling, chub, perch, or even with the dry fly in Hampshire, I would recommend a rod of ten feet six inches and of reasonable power and weight. With such a rod I have caught hundreds of trout, both with wet and dry fly, and dozens of salmon in the Scottish Dee.

Unless every shilling is of vital importance, there is little doubt but that a modern split-cane-built rod is the best in this size. But, if cheapness is an essential, buy rather a greenheart rod than an inferior split-cane rod. And be particularly wary of second-hand rods!

If you go to a good maker and tell him your needs he can usually be relied on to provide a rod entirely suitable for them.

All rods are, in a sense, compromises. On the one hand lightness is a desirable quality; but power and strength is an essential: stiffness and " punch " are wanted in a wind, but are most tiring in easy conditions. A quick action is pleasant for dry fly work, but is harsh if fishing a sunk line and often means broken casts when striking in wet fly-fishing.

So the "one-rod man" must accept the fact that his instrument will be perfect in no sense save that it will meet the demands of every occasion. And there are many, like myself, who prefer to stand by an old friend whose weaknesses are known and who is sympathetic to our own, than to ring the changes in attempting always to achieve the ideal for all conditions.

One rod, then, it shall be; and of a length of ten feet six inches. When buying this rod the salesman will almost certainly put it up in the shop and tell you to try the " feel " of it. There is not one person in a thousand who knows what to look for in this fatuous operation.

Very little indeed can be told from " trying the feel " of any rod. You may observe that it is straight—elementary but important—and perhaps that the cork handle is either too thick or too thin for your taste. You may see that the ferrules fit snugly and that the rings and bindings are in order. But of its casting virtues or vices you can tell very little unless you know what to look for.

Hold the rod in your hand parallel to the floor, and first, see how much bend there is in the rod top and middle joints under its own weight. It *should* bend slightly, especially in the lower part of the middle piece and at the top of the butt piece. Always mistrust a rod that shows no bend, as it is almost certain to be overstrong in the middle and butt pieces—and with such a rod all save very long lines are most difficult to throw.

The top joint, however, should under no circumstances show any bend. A top piece which bends under its own weight will never pick up a line from the water.

Now jerk the rod upwards sharply and watch the tip. It should appear to dip slightly before rising (due to the flexing of the middle joint before the top), and it should then spring very quickly upwards to a point well above the axis of the rod before returning to a true central position. It should *not* vibrate while doing this.

The object of these tests is to judge the strength and flexibility of the centre piece and the butt. It is from these that all the power in casting is derived and they must be neither too stiff nor too whippy. A top piece that is whippy is quite hopeless. A centre piece that is too stiff means that the top joint will be called upon for more work than it can do, while a butt that is too stiff means that both centre and top will be saddled with the work.

Too whippy a middle joint, on the other hand, means a soft powerless rod—but I have yet to come across a rod that is really too pliable in the butt. The feel of movement should, ideally, come right down into the handle itself, and in all the really good rods I have ever known one has the impression when casting that the cork rings forming the handle are actually moving over the wooden core as the rod flexes.

These remarks apply equally both to split-cane and to greenheart rods. But as a generalisation both will, on the whole, tend to be rather too weak in the middle joints than the reverse.

In consequence of this almost universal failing, the makers will recommend a line for use with the rod that is at least one size lighter than should normally be used. This guarantees the life of their rods! Have nothing to do with this. A ten foot six inch rod should throw a No. 5 "Kingfisher" if necessary, and a No. 4 with the greatest of ease. If the salesman tells you that a No. 5 is too heavy, then don't buy the rod but go elsewhere and try again.

If you are coaxed into buying and fishing with one of these very light lines, your life will be made miserable every time there is a breath of wind, and you will, at all times, have great difficulty in throwing a short or medium-short line at all satisfactorily.

The truth of the matter is that a rod and its lines are complementary and inseparable. When buying an outfit you should bear this in mind. A "good rod" automatically entails a line to fit it; and any rod, however good, that has the wrong line on it cannot appear other than indifferent.

A word or two about rod fittings may not be out of place. Nowadays the glue used to hold the individual lengths of bamboo together in a rod is so good that any binding of silk or cotton thread is no longer necessary. Many people were put off by the sight of an unbound split-cane because they are used to seeing the bound type. This is a pity since an unbound rod is necessarily lighter and has a greater power/weight ratio than the same rod bound.

In trout rods the question of rings is most important. The object of a ring is to hold the line near the rod and to act as a guide to it. Now rings have two disadvantages. Firstly, they are neither without weight or without friction, and secondly, unless placed so close together as almost to be touching they allow the line under tension to be pulled away from the rod except at the parts where the rings themselves are situated. They have the disadvantage, too, that when at the top of the cast and "waiting" a little slack line is apt to fall back through the rings and in so doing spoil the forward throw.

The ring, then, should (*a*) be as light as possible, (*b*) be as frictionless as possible, and (*c*) placed not so far apart as to prevent the line running freely if in a fish nor so close together as to add unnecessary weight to the rod.

Makers have many fads and idiosyncrasies about the type of rings they fit. The beginner would, however, be well advised to have nothing to do with any innovations or departures from the standard. The top ring of a rod should be a small agate or porcelain-lined bridge-ring. The bottom ring may likewise be a bridge-ring and, if required, also lined. But it *must* be big, otherwise when winding the line on to the reel it all piles on to one portion of it unless guided with the finger.

The intermediate rings should all be snake-rings. There is no substitute yet made which is as light and efficient, which is as strong and so trouble-free—and so cheap! Many makers have thought to improve upon them by fitting specially made bridge-rings. I do not think anyone who ever bought a rod so equipped would ever buy another. The first trouble with the intermediate bridge-rings is that if light enough, then they are very delicate and become injured at the slightest knock. The second, and by far the most serious, is that if fishing with grease on the line, bridge-rings quickly become furred up to such an extent as to prevent the line running through them. Snake-rings are very strong, very light and are self-cleaning to a large extent. Always insist on them for the intermediate rings.

I have seen trout rods made with "folding" rings which fall down against the rod when it was held upright. The idea was to prevent any dropping back of the line at the slack moment at the top of the cast. I do not think they were a success in this respect. And trying to put the line through them nearly drove me mad!

The next item is the reel. Do not be led astray by an enthusiastic salesman over this. The reel, properly speaking, plays no part whatever in fly-fishing. It is merely a mechanical device for taking up and holding the slack line you are not using at the moment and for letting it run when you do need it. As a machine the reel requires to fulfil three functions. It must hold sufficient line and backing for your purpose, i.e. thirty yards of tapered line and sixty yards of thin backing. It should preferably be narrow in the drum and rather big in circumference to give a quicker wind in; and it should have an adjustable check on the ratchet (preferable but not essential) so that its natural pull on the line can be suited to the strength of cast and size of fly you are using.

In short, provided a reel meets these requirements it is absolutely satisfactory for fishing with whatever its price and its substance.

The question of weight, however, limits the field somewhat. Without going into unnecessary detail it may be said that you cannot virtually have a reel that is *too* light. A heavy reel upsets the balance of any fly-rod and makes casting difficult. The consequence is that most fly-reels are made nowadays of duralumin. This metal is light and strong—but it has the unfortunate tendency to oxydize when wet. It should always, therefore, be dried off carefully.

It is always worth while paying a few extra shillings to buy a reel with a spare ratchet. These parts are subject to enormous wear and strain and have the unfortunate tendency to break when least expected: and nothing is more tiresome than trying to fish with a reel with a broken ratchet.

What is all this going to cost? A most important consideration. The answer is not easy to give; and as there is at present one variable which is quite unaccountable, namely purchase-tax, we had better make our reckoning without it. To our little budget will have to be added the percentage of purchase-tax ruling at the time.

The best split-cane rod would cost £1 per foot. A first quality silk line of thirty feet would cost 35s., and a really good reel with backing would run to about £3. Our ten foot six inch rod and accessories would then cost us, if of the first quality, rather over £15, *less purchase-tax*.

If this is excessive let us take an alternative:

Best quality spliced greenheart rod	£4 0s. 0d.
,, ,, silk line (essential)	£1 15s. 0d.
Reel adequate for work	£1 0s. 0d.
TOTAL	£6 15s. 0d.

Cheap lines are a false economy. Buy yourself the best fly-line in the market and look after it. If carefully dried after use, and if not kept on the reel, but loosely coiled and hung up in a dry, dark cupboard in the off-season it will last many years. Above all, do not buy a line that is too light for the rod or you will fish in discomfort all your life.

The possessor of a rod and line, you can now start practising casting. A lawn is not a bad place for a beginning. Tie a knot in the end of your line to prevent it fraying and then put your rod down and pull out about ten yards of line and lay it out on the grass straight in front of you. Then start to cast in the manner described earlier in the chapter.

If you can find a piece of water to practise on—a dew pond or a village pond, are perfectly adequate—the results will be even better. It is far easier to see if your line is going out straight on water than on grass, and you can also tell whether it is being thrown in with a heavy splash or if it falls in quietly after straightening out a few inches above the surface.

On water, you can, once the general idea of casting is mastered, try out some of the little tricks which help so much in fishing and most of which are quite easy to learn.

The first of these is " shooting " the line. This trick helps you to cast rather farther than the rod would normally do. The limit of distance a rod will cast is set by the length of line which it will pick up off the water and cast out *behind*, not in the amount of line it will throw forward. In other words, you can always throw more line forward than you can throw back; and, therefore, you can always throw the limit of what you can pick up with more energy forwards than is needed for that particular length of line. In " shooting " you make use of this fact by making the extra energy imparted to the line in the forward throw do the " work " of carrying an extra yard or two of line with it.

To " shoot " line, therefore, you first throw out a fairly long line. Then pull out another yard or two from the reel and let it hang in a loop from your finger which holds the line against the handle during the cast and prevents your slack loop passing through the rings. Make your back-cast and also the normal forward throw.

But as you complete this, let go of the line: it will then run through the rings as the line straightens and you will have cast a yard or two farther than you would otherwise have done. Before making another cast pull back the same length of line as you " shot " and hold it in a loop as before. Some people prefer to hold this loop in the left hand while making the cast. This is a matter of taste.

Another little trick which is very easy to learn and of untold value when trees interfere with normal casting (and usually this is where the best trout lie!) is to cast with the rod held nearly horizontally instead of vertically. The movements are precisely the same, but care must be taken to keep the end of the line and cast from hitting the water behind.

Even more useful is to acquire the knack of making some form of Spey or switch cast. This is surprisingly easy to do, but it is astonishing how few trout (and even salmon) fishermen ever master it. I will leave a description of this cast until we come on to salmon fishing.

Chapter XIV

WET FLY-FISHING FOR TROUT

FLY-FISHING for trout divides itself into two methods, wet fly-fishing and dry fly-fishing. In the former the angler uses flies which simulate food which the trout eats below the surface of the water; in the latter food which is taken floating on the surface itself. Before embarking upon instruction in these methods it is perhaps important that the fisherman should be clear in his mind as to what the feeding habits of the trout normally are.

The trout is essentially, as are most freshwater fish, a feeder on protein foods. These consist chiefly of (*a*) insects, and (*b*) small fish. In the winter, when the temperature of the water is low, the trout's own body temperature is low and the rate at which his metabolic processes function is also low: He requires, consequently, little food and, while in no sense starving, eats very moderately. At such times he confines his diet to small crustaceans such as shrimps and snails, and any occasional small fish which ventures within easy reach.

But with spring and the warming of the water in which he lives, and after the considerable drain on his resources of spawning in the winter, the trout becomes more active and more voracious. With spring, too, comes the awakening of new life in the water world. Insect larvæ which have been dormant throughout the winter and have lain, attached often to stones or weeds, hidden and motionless, now begin to hatch out into nymphs and flies. And these now form a very important addition to the trout's food. It is these nymphs and hatching flies on which the trout are feeding which the fisherman attempts to copy with his wet flies. And it is the completely hatched fly which has emancipated itself from its watery existence and which is either about to become airborne or is about to lay its eggs in the water again which the dry fly fisherman simulates with his lures.

Wet fly-fishing, then, is essentially a method of catching trout which are feeding either on shrimps or on the nymphs, or not fully hatched specimens of the " diptera " and " ephemeridæ ". Dry fly-fishing is a method of luring trout to destruction by presenting them with imitations of a fully hatched fly floating on the surface. It may, perhaps, seem elementary to point these facts out. Nevertheless, while the dry fly fisherman usually takes immense pains to fish a fly which, both in appearance and in behaviour, conforms as nearly as possible to the insects which he can see floating down the river, the average wet fly fisherman often has no idea at all what he is trying to imitate with his flies !

Fishing with the wet fly may be successfully employed in most waters where trout live. The exceptions we will leave for the moment until we come to the chapter on dry fly-fishing. Let us suppose that our fisherman has been given a day in April on one of our northern streams and is now getting together the tackle he requires.

His rod and line are already chosen and were described in the last chapter, as was also the way to use them in casting. He now needs a cast. This should be of the finest gut which he dares to fish with—" Fine and far off ", said Isaac Walton, " was the secret of successful angling." The cast should be at least three yards long and not thicker than of 2X gut (3X would be preferable, 4X perhaps dangerously light for a beginner). He wants to fish his flies below the surface, so, unless the stream is very sluggish, he will not require to grease his line to make it float. He will require a landing net which may be bought at prices varying from a few shillings to as many pounds : its only essential requirement is that it shall be large enough !

Armed with these he has everything necessary to fish with, save two items—his footwear and his flies. The former is of some importance. Even in very small streams it is sometimes an enormous advantage to be able to step into the water either to reach a fish or to free the line from an obstacle. A pair of rubber boots or thigh waders, while not essential, are often so useful that, in my opinion, they should never be left out of an angler's equipment.

What flies will he need? The literature upon this subject is enormous. It might be true to say that every fisherman has his own views upon which are the best flies, the best sizes, and the best changes, and so on. And if we examine the matter critically and remember the facts we have detailed in an earlier chapter as to the conclusion that within certain limits, it does not very much matter what patterns or even sizes of flies we use. The best fly for any fisherman is the fly in which he has most confidence; for this is the fly he will fish most carefully and lovingly!

Since, dear reader, you are (or should be!) a beginner, I am going to dismiss this matter very briefly with the advice to take with you but four patterns of flies, each of them in three sizes—twelve flies in all. When you have become an expert you will probably disagree violently with me both in the matter of choice of patterns and in the restricted number I have given. But in all honesty I can truthfully say that I would be perfectly happy to fish wet fly for trout anywhere and all my life with none other than these patterns and sizes.

Our choice, then, would be sizes o, 2 and 4 in the following patterns: March Brown (Female), Greenwell's Glory, Wickham's Fancy and Zulu.

Much difference of opinion exists to the number of flies that should be fished at the same time on the cast. Some experts fish as many as four flies at intervals of about eighteen inches on the cast. Others will fish but a single fly. And for each school of thought a few perfectly sound arguments exist. By fishing a variety of patterns and sizes at once, angler "A" says that his chances of tempting the trout with something to his liking are far greater than if he confined himself to a single fly. Very true, possibly, under certain conditions. Angler "B", on the other hand, says that too many flies following each other round at each cast may frighten the fish, that the trout will take a single fly more readily than one of a choice of three or four, that very often two trout will take flies at the same moment and break the cast, and lastly, that in a wind a number of flies on a cast often lead to tangles.

Personally, I side rather with angler "B" for a number of reasons, but mainly that I prefer to confine my attack upon a skilful adversary to tempting him with one fly at a time. The beginner should certainly not attempt to cast with more than two flies at once until his handling of the rod and line is competent.

Let us, therefore, compromise and fish with two flies. Now, clear in his intention, equipped in every important detail for his task, eager for the fray, our beginner arrives at the riverside, puts up his rod and ties on his cast. He looks at the sky and decides, as it is rather a bright morning, that he will use a March Brown as his tail fly and a Wickham's Fancy for the dropper. He ties on the tail fly with a figure of eight knot (as described in Chapter XXIV) and the dropper, about half-way up the cast. A mile of river lies before him—where is he to begin?

As it is still quite early in the morning he is not surprised to note that no rises are to be seen. The trout are not yet feeding at the surface and on fully hatched flies. They are still either nosing around in the little runs and stickles of the shallower stretches, feeding on such nymphs and larvæ as are carried down to them, or feeding in very deep water where a fly will not be noticed.

So he decides that the faster flowing streams will offer the best chance. Standing in the water at the head of a run he throws his line slightly downstream and lets the current carry his flies across until they land more or less straight below him. Whenever they pass through the little eddies behind the bigger stones he is particularly hopeful and expectant. And very soon his efforts are rewarded by a sharp pull which quickly develops into an erratic tugging at his line as the trout starts trying to make his escape.

On feeling the first pull our beginner may be tempted to lift his rod and pull against the fish. This is striking. And I say quite unequivocably that any attempt at striking when fishing the wet fly in running water is not only useless but absolutely wrong! By the time the pull of a taking fish has been felt he has either hooked himself or has got the fly out of his mouth. By striking you can only do one of two things: first you may pull the hook out of his mouth if it is not too secure in its hold, or second, you may break your cast.

I feel it only fair to say that there is a very considerable body of experts who consider it absolutely essential to strike immediately a trout is felt to take the fly. This, they say, "drives the hook home". I can only say that my own experience is that this is wrong.

In any event, whether you strike or not, you will have to get on terms with your trout as soon as possible. By this I mean raise the point of your rod nearly to vertical and thus lift all the slack line out of the water so that the stream cannot either pull on or deflect the angle at which you pull on the trout when playing him. Once this is done you are now so placed that you can exert the maximum of strain that the thickness of your cast will permit, and at the same time keep in hand, as it were, the ability to slacken off immediately by lowering your rod point if the fish makes a sudden rush away from you.

The art of playing a fish lies in tiring him out as quickly and as safely as possible. To do this it is necessary to make him do as much work as possible, especially with his fins which have small muscles only, while at the same time exerting a reasonably light pressure. In a river you have an ally in the force of the stream. If you keep his head always being pulled square across the stream towards you, you will make him struggle to keep on an even keel and also to remain with his head straight upstream.

Keep as nearly directly opposite your fish as you can, therefore. Be gentle in your handling of him, and if he suddenly decides to move away let him go until his run is ended and then tighten up on him again and pull him gently towards you. Sooner or later, according to his size, he will turn on his side, when the net can be put into the water and the fish pulled over its ring and into the centre. Then lift the net quietly and the trout is yours.

Never try to use the net like a scoop or ladle. Always put it into the water and *then* bring the trout into it.

This, our beginner's first brown trout, has behaved like a gentleman. He took the tail fly so that there was no caution necessary when netting him in case this fly caught up in a weed or rock while bringing him in. He did not run for a weed bed but fought cleanly and well in a strong stream. And *t*here he lies a full pound in weight (well, anyway, three-quarters of a pound even on the scales !). Look well at him now, my friend, in all his glory of gold and black. In a few hours he will be stiff and faded—just a rather dead fish—now he is the fulfilment of a dream.

As the day wears on and the sun strengthens, a few fleecy clouds begin to gather in the sky. Our angler now notices a few trout beginning to rise in the slower water of the deeper pools. He sees, too, some fully hatched flies, probably March Browns at this time of year, beginning to show in flight above the stream. He tries a cast over a rising fish, but notices that if he throws his flies slightly above the mark of the rise and lets them drift down over the fish, he gets a slight touch on his line followed by the sight of a deep boil on the surface made by the turning fish. And as a beginner he will, after failing to raise this fish again, try a second fish with identical results.

He may now, being an intelligent man, sit down for a moment and consider what has happened. His line of reasoning may run something like this.

" While I was fishing in the fast water the fish came at my fly and took it with a grab. I saw him rise at the same instant as I felt him on the line. Now in this slacker water he just seems to touch the fly, and I see the rise only some instants after I have felt him." Having analysed the position this far he would now quite rightly conclude that :

(*a*) In the slow water his flies were sinking perhaps too deep, hence the time-lag between seeing the rise and feeling the fish.

(*b*) That his flies were moving too slowly. That the trout had too much time to look at them, and could see that they were really rather poor imitations of the nymphs on which he was feeding.

So our intelligent angler does two things. First, he changes his flies to smaller sizes, since he considers that the trout will have more difficulty in discerning the difference between the artificial and the natural nymphs. Second, he decides that he must impart a little movement to them as the strength of the current does not give them enough. He does this by (*a*) lifting the point of his rod as the flies drift round, and (*b*) by pulling in handfuls of line at the same time.

Now he is rewarded. The next rising fish over which he casts makes no mistake. He grabs the tail fly with a bang and, securely hooked, pulls the slack line from between the fingers of our angler's left hand as he rushes off across the pool to seek shelter in the depths.

Several important lessons emerge from this imaginary morning's fishing; and they are so fundamental to all fly-fishing that it is well worth summarising them.

1. When wet fly-fishing for trout it is a golden rule that when the fish are not rising at the natural fly it is best to confine one's attention to the faster streams and shallower rocky or stony runs. Here there is always the chance of encountering a few trout nosing around and waiting for any tit-bit that the stream may bring them. In the deeper pools they are generally feeding on the bottom and are unlikely to come to the surface for your isolated flies.

2. You can afford to fish with comparatively large flies in fast water, especially if it is shallow, because the fish only get a passing glimpse of the fly as it sweeps over them, and because something slightly larger is more likely to attract their attention.

3. It is quite unnecessary to "strike" any fish in fast water. The speed at which the fly is moving at the end of a straight line ensures that if the fish pulls the fly he is either hooked or lost long before you, the angler, can do anything about it.

4. In slack water it is usually necessary to use smaller flies as the fish have much more time in which to examine the lure.

5. Similarly in slack water it is necessary to give some movement to the fly by raising the rod and pulling in line.

6. It is essential when pulling in line that, especially if striking, the line be lightly held between the fingers, otherwise a break is nearly sure if a big fish is encountered.

We have taken two somewhat extreme instances of different types of water when making our comparison. It will be realised, however, that between the very fast stickles and the almost streamless pool exists an infinite variety of type of water and that each stretch of a river must be examined and fished according to the merits and demerits of its own particular character.

It is perhaps true to say that it is their variety more than any other single factor which places the charms of fishing in moving water, in the estimation of nearly all fishermen, so far above those of fishing in still water. And fishing in a stream requires knowledge and experience which is generally known as " watermanship " and which is very difficult to define.

However fast a stream there are always little eddies and backwaters in it which may hold a fish. The experienced " waterman " will immediately recognise such places, and will concentrate on them. The inexperienced beginner has no option but to fish the whole of the stretch and, by noting the appearance of the places where fish have risen to his fly and taken it, learn to recognise likely places in this manner. No book can ever hope to describe this aspect of watermanship.

Similarly experience alone can teach the beginner the approximate speeds of currents from the appearance of the water and by the feel of the pull on his line. Such knowledge is, however, essential to successful wet fly-fishing if only for one reason. If a line is cast square across a current the effect, after a few moments, is to put a big curve into the line in the water as it swings round. This by itself is bad enough, because if a fish now takes the fly, instead of pulling against the rod and " striking " itself firmly on to the hook, it pulls against a yielding line which must be straightened out before the rod comes into action. Even worse, however, is the fact that as the curve, or " belly ", in the line gets more pronounced the flies at the end instead of swinging round gently in the stream, begin to be dragged across it at ever-increasing speed, until they are moving so fast that far from attracting the fish they merely scare them.

It is necessary, therefore, when fishing fast water, to cast far more at an angle downstream than when fishing slow water. And it is only " watermanship " which will tell you the right angle at which to cast your wet flies. In slow water you often require the added speed which a slight (not too great or you will merely " touch " and never hook fish) " belly " on the line gives the fly. In very fast water, even when casting at a slight angle to the stream, you cannot get your flies to move slowly enough across. Watermanship will inform you of this, and skill in "mending" the line will solve the problem.

"Mending" the line is an invaluable asset in all forms of fly-fishing in moving water. It is the trick by which the angler controls the speed at which his fly moves through the water. It is a trick which is generally held to be useful only in salmon fishing and which, consequently, few trout fishers ever master. But, be assured, it is invaluable, indeed essential, to competent and successful wet fly trout fishing. And it is simplicity itself. It consists merely in straightening out a belly on the line without disturbing the fly, or at times, in putting an upstream belly on the line to slow the fly down even more.

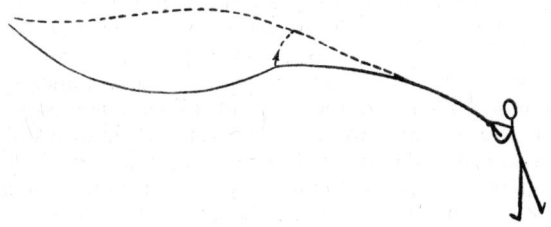

It is done with a slight movement of the wrist which moves the point of the rod up and round and down again in an arc of rather over half a circle and of a diameter varying from a few inches to perhaps a yard according to the amount of belly which it is required to "mend".

The diagram shows how the rod moves—and the line lifted off the water follows this movement in a snake-like motion.

Practise this, if necessary get some friend to demonstrate it to you. Together with accurate and able casting it will get you more trout in a season's fishing than all the gadgets that have ever been invented put together.

Chapter XV

LOCH FISHING FOR TROUT

Very different, yet with a charm and fascination peculiarly its own, is fishing for trout in the still waters of a loch or tarn. And because so many opportunities for this form of trout fishing exist even for those with the shallowest purses, it is probably one of the most commonly practised forms of trout fly-fishing in these islands.

The tackle required is perhaps somewhat different to that demanded by river-fishing. You can fish quite successfully in running water with rods as short as eight feet. But in still water, where all movement to the fly is imported by the motion of the rod, a short rod is at a grave disadvantage. The arc through which an eight foot rod is lifted is the same as that of a ten foot six inch or eleven foot rod. But the distance it draws the flies in is much less (actually some three feet), with the consequence that you fish a yard less water with every cast. Multiply this several hundred times in a day's fishing and the chances of catching trout will be seen to be much reduced.

The ten foot six inch general-purpose rod, however, will do admirably. The same line and reel will also suffice. But the size of flies used tends to be larger, though our four standard patterns could scarcely be bettered.

In a loch you may either fish from the bank, wade, or fish from a boat.

Fishing from the bank is not generally the most successful method. The trout tend to lie in the shallower water of the more gently sloping parts of the bottom, especially if there are weed beds growing on a shingle foundation. Where such favoured lies exist the nature of the slope of the loch floor prevents the bank fisherman from casting far enough to reach the best places. Where the bottom shelves away more deeply, however, the fisherman can easily cast into deep enough water—but the trout generally do not lie there.

If fishing from the bank, then, seek out some place where (*a*) the wind favours you by blowing from behind rather than into your face, (*b*) a headland or promontory exists from which you can cast into the bays on either side and into reasonably deep water.

Much the same considerations apply to the wading fisherman except that he is now much more favourably placed to cover rising and feeding fish. He will choose the same sort of water to fish in as the bank fisherman, but he will pay particular attention to the little weedy bays between promontories.

The style of fishing for both is the same. The object is to cover as much of the water as possible. The angler, takes up his stance, therefore, and starts to cast with a medium-length line. If on a headland he will cast perhaps a dozen times from the same spot and in a half-circle around him. Then he may draw off a yard or two more line and repeat the process. If fishing from a straight shore he may simply cast square ahead of him each time and take a step to one side before each new cast.

The speed at which he " fishes " his flies (i.e. draws them back through the water between casts) will materially affect the size of his bag. In quiet weather when little wind disturbs the surface he will need rather smaller flies, lighter casts, and will fish his flies fast through the water. When a good breeze disturbs the surface he can fish bigger, stronger and more slowly.

Distance, of course, is a material advantage. To cast a long line, to be able to hand-line a yard or two of it in before beginning to draw the flies up with the rod at all, and to be able to " shoot " the coil now drawn in at the next cast gives far greater chances than the mere casting of a medium-length line.

In still water it is quite essential to strike! And striking trout in a loch is not always easy. It is an operation requiring great delicacy of touch, since no two trout will take the fly in the same manner. Sometimes the fish will pull at the fly almost as soon as it hits the water. I have even seen them jump out to take the fly before it fell. On such occasions striking is easy and normal. A slight raising of the rod tip and the fish is hooked.

More often than not, however, the trout will follow the fly for some distance and only take it as it starts to accelerate as you begin the back-throw of your next cast. Now is a moment fraught with danger. If the fish takes very late, and if your tackle is fine, you will not be able to arrest the motion of your rod quickly enough and you will be broken. Quite often, especially with sea-trout in estuaries, you will give the fish such a jerk that the point of a greenheart rod will break! For this reason, if for no other, it is absolutely essential that the loch fisherman learns to fish at all times with a loop of line held lightly in the fingers of the free (left) hand. As a routine habit this will save hundreds of broken casts and lost flies and fish in a lifetime's fishing.

While there are certain times of day which, varying with the season, will always offer better chances than other times, it is fairly true to say that, with the exception of thundery periods, hope of catching trout in lochs need never be absent. Loch trout if feeding during the summer more avidly in the early morning and the late evening, nevertheless seem always prepared to accept a mouthful at any time of day. A hot, strong sun, except in the early spring, is liable to put them off, and the evening rise may be totally destroyed by frost or the rising of mist from the surface of the water. But generally speaking the only virtually hopeless condition is a total absence of wind—and this is hopeless, not because the trout do not feed, but because they can see too clearly all the paraphernalia of line, cast, knots and hooks which go to make up your tackle. If forced to fish in a flat calm there is usually but one hope. Grease your line, put on the finest cast you can find and tie on a single oiled dry fly. Cast this as far as you can and let it rest upon the water. *Sometimes*, after a few minutes, an inquisitive trout will come up and take it. More often they will rise to, but never touch, the fly.

For wading in still water a pair of thigh boots is usually sufficient, and they are a great deal less cumbrous than trouser waders. But be doubly wary of boots with rubber soles. Even when amply ridged these slip in a terrifying manner on every stone. Always get boots with either nailed or felted soles.

Boat-fishing on lochs for trout can be great fun. It can also be astonishingly tedious. The tedious method of fly-fishing from a boat can shortly be dismissed. It is not fishing. It consists of hanging your rod over the stern with about forty yards of line out with the cast and flies on the end of it. The boat is then rowed by yourself or by a boatman at a fair walking pace and it is hoped that some trout will come and attach himself to a fly, when the boat is stopped and he is landed.

On a fine sunny day this form of " sport " is pleasant provided (*a*) it is warm enough to sit inactive in comfort, (*b*) the seat is comfortable, (*c*) someone else rows the boat, (*d*) you either are a good sleeper or have a good book to read. It is unpleasant if all these requirements are not fulfilled and sheer undiluted misery if none of them are.

Drifting and casting, however, if intelligently done, can be a profitable and pleasurable experience. First the direction of the wind is noted. Then the boat rowed to the windward end of the loch and a strip of water down which the boat will drift, if left to its own devices, is chosen so that it covers as many likely banks and shallows as possible. It is then turned broadside to the wind, and as it starts to drift, the angler starts fishing in identically the same manner as from the shore or wading. Now, however, the boat has a certain speed which must be taken into account when drawing the flies towards you. And if the wind is at all strong and the boat is going fast, it means a quick recovery and casting that is too quickly repeated for comfort. It is often well worth putting out either a stone on the end of a rope which drags on the bottom, or else a bucket or a proper sea-anchor to prevent the boat drifting too quickly.

In general, too, it is well to remember that it is the bays and inlets quite close to the shore, or the banks near islands that offer better chances than the depths in the open water of big lochs. It is a nuisance sometimes to have to row about to new short drifts; but it pays a better dividend to do this than to take a long drift over unsuitable water.

In a very strong wind life is made very easy. It becomes unnecessary to cast at all. Merely draw the rod up to vertical and give it a little roll forward. The wind will do the rest and take the line and cast out perfectly.

Chapter XVI

DRY FLY TROUT FISHING

THERE has grown up over the years a legend about dry fly-fishing for trout which neither reason nor factual example can seriously break down. It is that only the most skilful fishermen, armed not only with the finest of rods and tackle, but also festooned with a variety of gadgets and possessed of the wisdom and experience of years of angling can hope to achieve success with the dry fly.

This is arrant nonsense. The truth of the matter is that anyone who can cast reasonably well, who uses a modicum of intelligence and who takes the trouble not to show himself too obviously to feeding trout can compete quite successfully with the self-styled expert. I would hazard that, by and large, catching feeding trout on the dry fly is perhaps the simplest of all forms of fly-fishing. But in fairness I must add that few will agree with me!

Nevertheless, the beginner would do well to approach dry fly-fishing in the belief that it is as easy as I suggest. He will at least then start under no handicap of having a complex about it.

In all forms of wet fly-fishing the object is to lure trout to destruction by presenting them with a bait which resembles either a larva, a nymph or some small crustacean or water insect. That the trout will take, say, a " zulu " fly in mistake for any of these should give the angler a clear indication of both the powers of vision and discernment of a trout, and of his intelligence!

Yet, for some reason unknown to me, the moment the dry fly is suggested, it is at once assumed that only the most perfect replicas of the fully hatched insect on which the trout is now feeding will suffice to catch him.

The dry fly, then, represents one of a score or more of insects, most of them of the Dipteræ or Ephemeridæ families which, having lived their larval and nymph stages in the water, have now undergone their last transformation and have emerged into the air as fully fledged winged flies whose one function remains to propagate their own species. After emerging from their last larval case the majority rest on the surface of the water for periods varying from a few seconds to many minutes for the purpose of drying and setting their wings before rising on a nuptial flight.

It is on these newly hatched insects that the rising trout will feed, and it follows to reason that if we would catch them we must present them with a lure which in appearance and behaviour has the same characteristics as these insects.

The first thing to note about them is that all of these natural flies sit on top of the water and not in it. They support themselves on the skin or surface of the river and on the points of their feet. The second thing to note is that, when sitting there, with few exceptions, they remain quite immobile except for the stretching of their wings. They do not, in general, propel themselves about the surface but merely drift and are carried down with the current.

Our artificial fly must, therefore : (*i*) float on the surface and not half-way through it ; (*ii*) remain motionless relative to the water while it is " fishing ".

We achieve these objects firstly by using a plentifully hackled fly with a small light hook ; we oil the fly and it does not, therefore, break through the surface of the water ; secondly by casting it upstream and allowing it to float down as far as possible without guidance or drag from the rod or line.

It will be seen, then, that certain modifications in our tackle are necessary for dry fly-fishing. The experts will tell you that a special type of light, quick-actioned rod is necessary. This is an over-statement. The fact is that in order to keep the fly dry it is necessary to make a false cast (i.e. throw the fly forwards and backwards without allowing it to alight upon the water) between casts and that a light rod with a somewhat stiffer action is less tiring to use than a heavier, softer rod. But the latter will do the work quite adequately. Also, it is preferable to use a somewhat lighter line since it must be greased and must float—and for this a smaller and lighter rod is to be preferred. But again it is in no sense a necessity.

Our rod, then, at best, will be a nine foot six inch light and stiff split-cane. But if this is not one of our possessions, the ten foot six inch general-purpose rod will be quite adequate.

The line should preferably be a size lighter than we would normally use for wet fly-fishing; but again this is an optimum, not a necessity. It must, however, be tapered.

The cast should be at minimum nine feet long and it is better to use a tapered cast with the tip as fine as 4X if you dare fish as fine as this.

In discussing the question of flies we are up against every conceivable form of prejudice and preference. The " real expert " will tell you that no dry fly fisherman is complete without dozens of different patterns in a score of sizes and styles of tying. There is an enormous literature on dry flies for trout and on the entomology of the natural insects. To attempt to cover the ground in a book for beginners would not only be impossible but also confusing.

I propose, therefore, to attack the problem from an entirely different and, I hope, rational angle. What is the trout really seeking, and what really are his powers of discrimination?

There is little doubt that when a big hatch of March Browns, such as is common in April on most rivers, appears on the river the trout rise to and eat them voraciously. There is little doubt also that, at such times, March Browns are what the trout are looking for. It is generally agreed, too, that a well-tied artificial March Brown properly cast over a rising fish will usually be taken. On the other hand it is true to say that any one of an enormous range of other artificial flies of *about the same size* will also be equally readily taken!

Can it be, then, that the trout either does not know or cannot see the difference? Here I think lies the key to the whole problem. If you are prepared to invest the trout with (*a*) the powers of vision which enable him to detect the exact shape, colour and detail of an insect sitting above the surface of the water and outlined against the sky while he remains beneath the surface, (*b*) the powers of thought and intelligence which can translate such abnormally acute visual reception into an ability to discriminate between an imperfect and a perfect replica of what he is seeking, then you cannot fish the dry fly until you are satisfied that you have an exact copy of every natural fly on which the trout may feed in your possession.

I, for one, am not prepared to invest the fish with these powers, and experience has satisfied me that neither in powers of vision nor in ability to reason does the trout anywhere approach the perfection generally attributed to it. Apart from the facts already stated that the fly must float, and must do so freely and without drag, only two things seem important to me. One is that it should be of about the same size and shape as the natural insect, and the other that it should be of the same tone (not necessarily colour) as the natural insect.

This is heresy let me assure you ; and it will be laughed to scorn by the experts. Nevertheless, it is a far less troublesome and every bit as successful approach to dry fly-fishing than the detailed instructions usually given in several hundred pages. And since I have found it completely satisfactory in results, let us carry our conclusion further and evolve a method.

Dry flies I divide up into five sizes. They are in descending order.

A Exceptionally big corresponding to Mayfly.

B Big corresponding to Stone Flies, March Browns, etc.

C Medium corresponding to Grannoms, Sedges, etc.

D Small corresponding to Spinners, Uprights, Duns, Olives, etc.

E Very small corresponding to Midges, Gnats, etc.

I also divide each size (except "A") into three tones :

1. Dark   2. Medium.   3. Light.

And each has two types of body :
               (*a*) Dull   (*b*) Bright

It follows, then, that with twenty-five different flies you are, under this system, completely equipped as a dry fly fisherman for every river in Britain and for every season of the year. We can, using these prefixes to denote them, make a table of our twenty-five flies, and since you are unlikely to be tying your own for some time, put the names of suitable patterns and sizes against each:

A   Mayfly

B
- 1
  - *a* Baigent's Black   No. 3 and 4
  - *b* Alder   ,,
- 2
  - *a* March Brown   ,,
  - *b* Greenwell's Glory   ,,
- 3
  - *a* Red Variant   ,,
  - *b* Pale Olive   ,,

C
- 1
  - *a* Baigent's Black   No. 1 or 2
  - *b* Alder   ,,
- 2
  - *a* March Brown   ,,
  - *b* Greenwell's Glory   ,,
- 3
  - *a* Red Variant   ,,
  - *b* Pale Olive   ,,

D
- 1
  - *a* Iron Blue   No. 0 and 00
  - *b* Dark Olive   ,,
-
  - *a* Greenwell's Glory   ,,
  - *b* Red Quill   ,,
- 3
  - *a* Dun Midge   ,,
  - *b* Pale Olive Spinner   ,,

E
- 1
  - *a* Black Gnat (male)   No. 000
  - *b* Black Gnat (female)   ,,
- 2
  - *a* Dun Midge   ,,
  - *b* Gold Ribbed Hares Ear   ,,
- 3
  - *a* Iron Blue Spinner   ,,
  - *b* Pale Watery Dun (male)   ,,

This list does not pretend to be any better than any of a dozen or more other lists which could equally well be made out. But it will serve as a guide to the sort of variations of flies which it is useful to have.

Grease or oil both for the line and for the fly will be required. I suggest that a tin of " Mucilin " is as satisfactory as any brand and better than most.

On arriving at the river and having set up your rod, run about fifteen yards of your line out and grease it well with a grease pad. It *must* float properly. Now clean your hands well and take a soaked tapered cast and attach it to the line, taking special care to see that no grease gets on to it. Should this happen it can quite well be cleaned off by rubbing it with a clean dock leaf. Now take a look around you and at the river. Any rising fish is obviously feeding. Watch him for a while and see if you can decide the sort of size and tone of the fly he is going for. Also see if you can see any of the type of flies trout usually feed on either sitting on the surface or flying about. You may not have seen any fish rising, but you may notice one or two lying quite close to the surface. These, also, are either feeding or fish which are just about to feed. You should not forget that any fish which you can see can also see you—so use some circumspection when making your reconnaissance.

Having found a stretch or a pool where there are one or two fish either rising or about to feed; and having decided on the sort of fly they are taking, you choose a suitable counterpart from your box and tie it on to the cast. Then remembering that you have got to float your fly down to the fish without any drag, you approach, either carefully along the bank or wading in the river, from below him, i.e. downstream. When you have reached a point which seems well within your reach start to pay out line.

Do not at first cast towards the fish. Take some point in another direction which seems about the same distance away as the fish and draw off line until you have got about five to six feet more than is required to reach it. Now turn towards the rising fish and very carefully cast your fly a yard or so above him so that the fly will float down through the centre of the ring of the rise. If you have done this gently and without a splash, and if your line is not *too* straight so that any little eddy between you and the fly causes a drag, the fly should float down perfectly to him and he should come up and take it first time.

If he fails to do so give him a minute or so and then try again. Provided you do not frighten him either by showing yourself or by splashing the line over him, and supposing always that you have picked a fly reasonably resembling in size and tone the natural insect he is eating, this trout is usually certain to take you in time.

When he does you will see him long before you feel him, and the problem that now arises is how to hook him. You have been casting upstream and letting the fly float down towards you. If you do this and take no steps to prevent it, your line will float downstream from the point of your rod in a big belly turning back again up to the fly. It is obvious, then, that you must, as the fly floats down, firstly draw in part of the slack through the rings and then, when you have as much as you can manage to " shoot " at the next cast, lift the point of the rod to take up the remainder. By doing this you can let your fly float a considerable distance before it is necessary to cast again. And, by ensuring that it does float well down below a rising fish, which does not immediately take, you run no risk of frightening him when lifting the line and fly off the water for another cast.

When the fish takes, then, you have your fly so much under control that a small lift of the point of the rod is sufficient to make contact, that the strike can be made.

After taking out your fish, see that the knot of your fly is all right. Dry it carefully by false casting several times and re-grease it. Then sit down for a moment and look for another feeding fish.

To the good and accurate caster who can take the trouble not to show himself (or his rod) to rising fish, catching trout on the dry fly is in most streams absolute child's play. The fun lies in fishing for a definite trout and in stalking and hooking him. Occasionally the casting is made difficult either because of overhanging trees (the " whales " always seem to lie under branches) or because the approach has to be made by crawling. This adds to the thrill and pleasure.

Sometimes very few rising fish are seen. But it is not necessary to give up fishing. In chalk streams and many of the shallower rivers every individual trout can be seen if careful search is made from the bank. By casting repeatedly enough over a place where a good fish is known to be lying it is often possible to deceive him into thinking that a hatch of fly is "on"; and eventually he will very probably come up and take you.

Often you cannot fish from below a particular trout. Usually a cast from the side can be made. At worst it may be necessary to cast from directly above him. In this case a straight line is fatal. The line must be cast so that it falls in "kinks" and the fly can float freely downstream while the kinks straighten themselves out. But in such circumstances it is first time or never. Recovering the line for another cast will put any fish down.

If I have simplified—over-simplified many will say—the art of dry fly-fishing for trout and condensed the necessities into a short chapter, it has been done for a purpose. Experience alone can teach the finer points. I have told you as much as a beginner needs to know or can usefully assimilate without much experience. And if you read one of the hundreds of treatises on this form of fishing you will probably be so appalled by its endless technicalities that you will probably shelve the whole matter as beyond you.

Perfect your casting. Keep out of sight. Remember what the fish is thinking and also his limitations of vision and intelligence, and unless your observations of the flies he is taking and your efforts to match them in size and tone are very bad you are certain to get your fair share of the bag.

Before leaving this chapter a word must be said about mayflies. On most southern rivers and a few northern there appears in May or June a large insect known as the mayfly. The trout now go completely mad and devour them avidly for several days. At such times every trout in the river, big and little, seems to be feeding. And they also seem to lose all sense of fear and all guile.

By impaling two natural insects on a hook and "dapping" them on to the surface with a long rod trout can be caught in large numbers. By tying an artificial mayfly and casting in the normal manner a similar result is achieved.

I do not call this fishing; yet many of our richer brethren never approach the river at all until the keeper telephones them that the mayfly is on. It is perhaps an experience worth having once. But it is all too easy to be called real fishing.

Chapter XVII

TROUT FISHING—OTHER METHODS

WHILE fly-fishing is unquestionably the happiest and most satisfactory method of taking trout, other ways exist which require much skill and which, in unsuitable fly conditions, may be the only ones offering any chance of success.

Of these, spinning is probably the most popular. It has the undoubted satisfaction, too, that almost every trout caught on a spinning bait is either already, or shortly will become, a cannibal: and as such is lost as a sporting fish to the fly fisherman.

Modern spinning for trout is almost invariably carried out with thread-line tackle. This entails a short, light rod of not more than six feet in length. These are generally of split-cane manufacture, but the steel rod is gaining daily in popularity. The reel is either of the fixed-spool type (Illustration No. 1), such as the Illingworth (the original of these) or one of the many designed by most tackle-makers on the same principle: or else it is of the wide narrow spool type such as the Pfleuger type.

1

Both types of reel allow a very light bait to be cast great distances with little effort. The lines are either of fine braided silk or of gut substitute and usually have a breaking strain of only a few pounds. To the fisherman who envisages much spinning for trout the expense of a rod, reel and line of this type, though considerable (over £20 to-day), is a worth-while outlay. But the want of such tackle does not necessarily preclude an occasional afternoon's spinning. A light "Nottingham" reel with a thread-line can very well be used off a fly-rod, and in the hands of a master can produce every bit as good results as a proper thread-line spinning outfit. In the old days, too, trout spinning was invariably practised with the ordinary fly-fishing tackle. The line was drawn off the reel to a length of about twenty yards and was either coiled in the left hand or laid on the ground at the angler's feet. Then holding the bait drawn well up to near the top ring it was cast out and the free line allowed to pass through the rings as the bait sailed away. The bait was " spun " and the line recovered by hand-lining. This method works perfectly well after a little practice.

Whatever tackle and method you are using the principles of spinning remain the same. This is *par excellence* the means of catching trout in slightly dirty water when the river is in spate or in cold weather when the fish are not showing to the fly. It is an excellent way of catching those monsters which live in the deeper pools and which never come to the fly at all; and as such may be, if not overdone, an unqualified benefit to the river in ridding it of those most undesirable characters, the big cannibals.

Baits may be either natural or artificial. Natural baits usually include minnows, small loach or gudgeon, and shrimps. Without exception these are all most effective if freshly killed and have not lost their colour by being preserved. They are mounted usually either on an " archer " type mount (Illustration on page 50) or on a lip-hook mount (Illustration, " Wagtail ", page 64). Best of all, however, I consider the scarab mount. This is a transparent sheath of celluloid having the fins attached. The bait is placed within the sheath and is bound in place with fine copper or silvered wire.

One pattern of hook I consider so superior to all others for small spinning triangles that I would suggest that every effort should be made to acquire them. These are the "Illingworth" type of hook with the barb on the very point of the hook itself.

Personally I favour the use of a single triangle at the tail of the bait rather than two or more spaced along its length.

Natural baits require some added weight. Either this can be attached to the cast about eighteen inches above the bait, or it can be in the form of a mouth-lead which is inserted in the bait itself. These latter are the better type. The illustration (No. 2) shows how this type of tackle is used and how the hooks are mounted. The bait, together with its lead, should not weigh more than one ounce unless very deep spinning is desired.

Artificial baits are normally either Devon minnows, phantom minnows or spoons (see Illustrations No. 3, 4 and 5). Devon minnows should be fished without leads. The others require sufficient lead to make casting possible. Leads should be either of the non-kink, spiral or simple lead wire type.

The cast or trace should be about two feet in length and should have two swivels at intervals in its length. It is useful to have a spring clip at the bait end for easy attachment. Otherwise a plain loop threaded through the eye of the hook mount and pulled back over the bait is perfectly satisfactory.

You will probably start your spinning in one of the deeper less streamy stretches of the river, or in a loch. First cast the bait at an angle of about 45 degrees across and downstream and wind in slowly as the bait swings round in the current (if in a river). Next try a cast more squarely across. To prevent the bait sinking and catching on the bottom you will have to wind in faster. Often you can very successfully cast upstream and wind the bait in very fast. When they will look at nothing else trout will sometimes take a spinning bait fished in this manner very freely.

Shrimp-fishing requires perhaps a slightly different technique. The shrimp can either be used on a mount just as with a minnow, or else it can be mounted on a single hook to gut threaded through the bait from head to tail so that the hook lies amongst the whiskers (see Illustration No. 6). Boiled shrimps should be used for this method. The shrimp thus mounted is now cast with as little lead as can be handled, upstream, and is allowed to sink to the bottom. As soon as it is felt to touch bottom, a small jerk lifts it off again and it is carried downstream again until once more it hits the bottom. The process is then repeated. This " sink and draw " method is particularly successful in clean warm water of reasonable speed. It is also, incidentally, a very deadly method of catching sea-trout and salmon in low water.

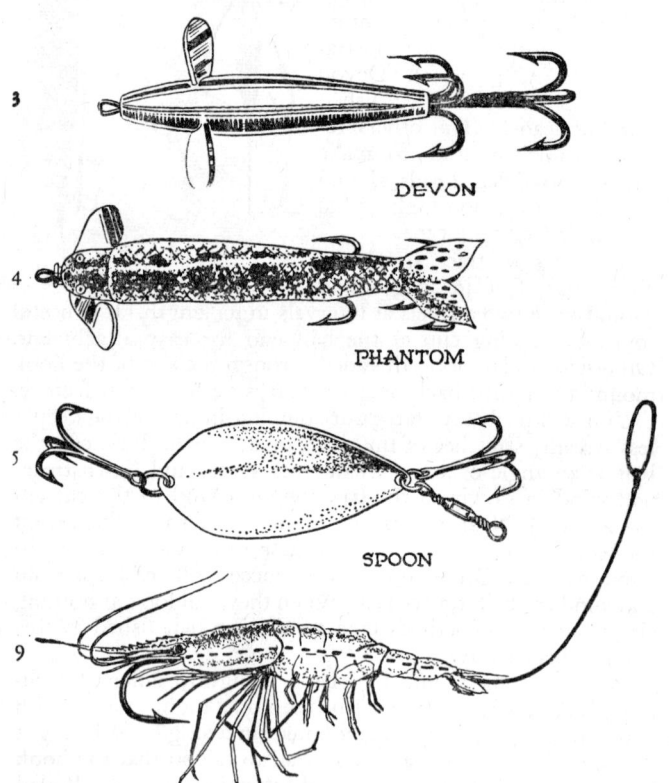

3 DEVON

4 PHANTOM

5 SPOON

9

Chapter XVIII

WORM-FISHING FOR TROUT

To the dry fly purist, the man who spins for trout, is almost beyond the pale. The lowest depths of degradation, however, are reserved for him who confesses to worming for trout.

Why this should be I have never been able to discover. I am not over fond of spinning myself, and find it not only dull but a somewhat laborious and unskilful method of fishing. But to fish the worm well not only demands the very highest degree of skill, but can be at the same time the most thrilling of all forms of trout fishing.

The technique is different in river and loch. Let us start with loch-fishing as it is somewhat simpler.

The way *not* to fish a worm is with a float as in coarse fishing. This is sometimes practised, not unsuccessfully, in mill ponds and the like; but it is a method which neither in skill nor in results is comparable to the casting and drawing method.

Comparatively shallow water is necessary for all forms of worm-fishing. By this I mean that it should be shallow enough to allow the bait to sink to the bottom in reasonable time. Twelve feet is probably the limit of depth, six to eight feet possibly the best depth.

A single hook to gut is to my mind better than a Stewart Tackle (Illustrations No. 7 and 8), and this should be attached to a fairly stout cast. The cast can be fished either from a spinning-rod, or preferably, from a fly-rod. On to the cast are punched a few lead shots and a well-scoured worm or two are threaded on to the hook.

If fishing with the fly-rod draw off a few yards of line and cast the worm out into deeper water as if spinning. Now wait for a few moments until the bait is felt to touch the bottom. Then very gently draw the worm back towards the bank or boat, never moving it so fast that it comes more than an inch or two off the bottom. While doing this allow it to rest every now and then for a few seconds.

In weedy water great skill is required to keep the bait from becoming entangled and it may be necessary under such circumstances not to allow it to sink below the level of the weeds.

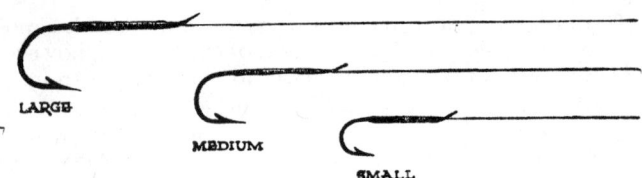

FINE WIRE TROUT WORM HOOKS

Trout may take a worm fished in this manner in many different ways. Sometimes they grab it with a powerful tug and hook themselves immediately. Then it is easy. At other times they merely stop the progress of the bait and can be felt very delicately mouthing it. Now the angler must, while keeping contact with the bait, be very careful not to pull it away from the fish and must be sure of giving it time to take the worm and hook well into its mouth before striking. The signal to do this is usually the fact that once he has properly a hold of it the trout is felt to make off with your hook. Often the trout will carefully eat the whole worm and leave you after perhaps a minute with an absolutely bare hook.

No description can convey the sense of excitement that this form of fishing can give. Were it not for the "messiness" and comparative inaction I would prefer worm-fishing for trout to all other methods.

THREE-HOOK "STEWART" WORM TACKLE

In the running water of a river worm-fishing can be even more exciting. Now the "sink and swim" principle of shrimp-fishing is employed. The bait is cast upstream with as little lead as possible and allowed to sink to the bottom. The stream now carries it down while contact is maintained by drawing in line. Every now and then the bait will come to rest. Leave it for a moment and tighten up very gently. If no movement is felt it is probably wedged on the bottom and a slight lift of the rod top suffices to free it. If, on the other hand, a slight tapping is felt it is a fish that has stopped it and is mouthing the worm.

Now comes the difficult part. You must at all times keep in touch with your bait, but you must not pull the line and hook away from the fish. And in running water this requires great delicacy of touch. After a while you will see your line beginning to move away upstream. This may be in a second or two after first feeling your fish, or it may not be for as much as a minute. When you see this, but not before, strike and you will have him.

In low, clear water, especially if it is a bright sunny day and the water is warm, this upstream worm-fishing can be the greatest of fun. It is usually best to wade and to work your way upstream through the rather more rapid shallow parts of the river.

The hook should be small and the worm small and of good colour. You can probably see most of the trout you will be fishing for lying in the eddies behind stones. It requires no small degree of skill to cast a worm so that it will be swept down into these eddies, and with so wary a fish in low, clear water, the utmost delicacy of touch to determine when the bait has been properly taken.

Do not, my friend, despise worming for trout whatever you do. Try it, and I guarantee that when you have mastered the art you will have some of the most enjoyable fishing of your life.

Chapter XIX

SALMON FISHING

You may be under the common delusion that salmon fishing is the prerogative of the very wealthy. It is not. True, it is that for the best beats of the best rivers fantastic rents are paid; that for even a bad beat of a poor river sums are given which bear no relationship to the value of the sport expected. Nevertheless, there is a quantity of absolutely free salmon fishing in these islands, an even greater amount on association water to which members may subscribe as little as two guineas a year and fish to their hearts' content, and a surprising amount that can be had with a daily or weekly ticket varying from £1 per day down to a guinea a month. In Scotland I know of one beat on one of the three best rivers where anyone staying as a visitor in a certain village may have free fishing; and I have seen eighty fish killed in a fortnight on this beat, one man having over twenty-five salmon to his own rod.

If you are going to take up fishing as a lifetime's hobby you will be virtually certain at some time or another to have an urge to catch the noblest of all our game fish, the salmon. Do not let the question of finance deter you. If you can afford the journey, and if you can buy, beg or borrow the necessary tackle, seek out some good fishing within your means and devote a holiday to it. If you catch but one fish the memory of it will sustain you for the rest of your days.

Like trout, salmon can be caught in three (legal!) ways: by fly-fishing, by spinning and on the worm. Fly-fishing, which is the subject of this chapter, again is divided into two methods: the sunk fly, which is used in the early spring and, often in the autumn, and greased-line fishing, which is practised in the late spring and summer. Since the techniques and the tackle are entirely different for each method of fishing we shall deal with them separately.

But first it is necessary to know something about the salmon, for without a knowledge of the singular behaviour of this fish throughout his life it is not possible to fish for him intelligently.

So far every fish we have been discussing in this book has been either a sea fish living in salt water or a freshwater fish living in a river, lake, canal or pond. Each of these, too, can be caught by proffering to it some bait which it takes as food and because it is in some degree hungry.

The salmon can be classed neither as a sea fish nor a freshwater fish, but it is a mixture of both; and since he does not feed in fresh water the bait with which he is lured can hardly be classed as food or imitation food!

The salmon is born in the river, usually in the headwaters where the stream is fast and the water pure. After hatching out in about the month of March the young fish lives on or near the "redd" or spawning bed in which his egg was deposited for several months. He then moves downstream and, unless the food supply—he has the same requirements as a young trout—is exceedingly good he will remain in the river throughout that winter, the following summer and succeeding winter. The average parr, as he is now known, lives for two years in the river. In rivers where the feeding is exceptionally good, such as the Hampshire Avon or the Test he probably only remains one year. Where the feeding is very poor he may remain three, four or even five years. The time he stays in the river as a parr seems determined by his rate of growth. As soon as he has reached a length of about four and half inches he will leave the river the following spring.

During April and May from every river which holds salmon a stream of young fish, now called smolts, issues forth to the open sea. While parr they look like young trout, but on becoming smolts they put on a silver dress and become miniature salmon.

For from eighteen months to three or sometimes four years they remain at sea. Eventually, all those that are left—about five per cent of those which start out—return to the same river as they were born in. No one can tell how they find their way home nor why an individual does not return to a river other than that in which he was born. No one knows where they go to or on what they feed while at sea. From the moment the little fish of perhaps two ounces leaves the river-mouth until he returns a year or two later, weighing anything from seven pounds upwards, the chapter in his life story is blank.

It will be realised that the salmon is a very remarkable fish. He is equipped with gills and kidneys which, once his silver coat is donned, will function equally well in fresh or salt water. He feeds voraciously as a parr and while at sea; but as soon as he comes back to the river a full-grown salmon he not only ceases entirely to feed, but his whole digestive processes undergo radical alteration and it is very doubtful if he would even be capable of feeding.

Nevertheless, he takes a fly or a bait quite readily. Many propositions as to why he does this have been put forward. The most likely is that while at sea he has grown so much into the habit of feeding on certain specific objects that immediately he sees the likeness of one, and in circumstances which recall the memory of feeding, he is liable to fall back into the custom of long-standing habit and go for it.

The salmon may enter our rivers at any time between December and the following November. Those that come early and those that come late all spawn roughly at the same time—in November and early December—and having spawned, almost all the males and about eighty to ninety per cent of the females die. The remainder make their way back to the sea in the spring floods of the following season where, if they are lucky, they fatten up and return again to spawn.

Fly-fishing for salmon in most British rivers from the opening of the season until about the middle of April is generally confined to sunk-line fishing.

The tackle you will require for this is specialised and it is unlikely that any of your coarse or trout outfit will fill the bill. The rod should be, at a minimum, thirteen feet six inches long and should be either of split-cane or a good greenheart. The reel should be of three and three-quarters to four and a quarter inches diameter, and should hold forty yards of line plus at least a further sixty yards of strong backing. Otherwise the quality of the reel is of no importance provided it has a ratchet and is in " working " condition.

The line should be heavy. A No. 6 " Kingfisher " or its equivalent would be right for a thirteen foot six inch to fourteen foot rod; but a No. 5 might just do if a No. 6 was not procurable.

You will be fishing with flies from two and a quarter to three inches long. You need, therefore, a very stout gut cast. For early spring fishing you cannot have one that is too thick. But to-day the heaviest gut cannot be bought and it is doubtful whether a cast with a diameter of more than .020 inches exists. Anything with the description of "medium" or "stout" salmon will probably suffice.

It is all too easy to overload oneself with unnecessary salmon flies. During a lifetime I have, for instance, bought literally several hundred flies, for one reason or another, which I have never used and am never likely to. To-day I confine myself to about four patterns and, for sunk-line fishing, never vary the size! I have found that salmon which take the sunk fly behave as though they were looking for some small fish which probably forms their normal sea food and which is of a particular size—i.e. about two and three-quarter inches. When fishing bait in the spring the size is seldom varied; so, I ask, why vary the size of the fly? This approach to the problem has proved highly successful in my own case and those of my friends who have followed my advice, and I have no hesitation in recommending you, dear reader, to do the same. It will not only simplify your fishing, but make it infinitely cheaper. A salmon fly costs anything from 7s. to 12s. 6d. to-day!

Of flies, therefore, confine yourself to a few patterns and all of approximately the same size, an 8/0. I would suggest that with the following flies you are completely equipped for every eventuality.

1. Ackroyd.
2. Thunder and Lightning.
3. Mar Lodge.
4. Silver Grey.

The Ackroyd, the "poor man's Jock Scott", as it is called, is the ideal general-purpose fly. It is invariably the fly I try first unless some circumstance dictates a darker or a lighter fly.

In choosing a salmon fly to try down a pool we are in somewhat the same position as when choosing a trout fly.

We want to present the fish with an artificial lure which in size and general tone represents the creature he is expecting to see. If, therefore, it is a very bright day and the water is clean, a dark fly looks too black to be a little fish. A bright fly alone is of the right " tone " relative to its surroundings to give this impression. On a dull day, conversely, a bright fly is too light when seen against the surrounding water and sky. A dark fly alone gives the correct impression.

Our four flies are chosen in a range of tone suitable to most conditions of light. The Ackroyd is a " medium " fly suitable for most conditions except the extremes. The Thunder and Lightning is a dark fly for a dull day, the Mar Lodge is a fairly bright fly for a bright spring day, and the Silver Grey is a very bright fly for a glaring day and very clear water.

Besides your rod, line, cast and flies there are two other specialised articles of equipment you will require. The first is a pair of trouser-waders with brogues. You may not always need to wade; often you can fish from the bank or from a boat. But inevitably in time you will be fishing where wading is a necessity. The second is a gaff with which to land your fish.

Casting with a double-handed salmon rod is precisely the same in principle as casting with a single-handed trout rod. Beyond the warning that the trout fisherman tends to use his wrists too much and his arms and body too little, there is no advice that would be helpful save to take your rod, if a novice, out on to the lawn and practise casting with it before you go down to the river. You may find the slower action somewhat strange; you will undoubtedly find the exercise unusual and, at first fatiguing. But if you can throw a trout line, you can also perfectly well throw a salmon line with a few minutes of practice and of accustoming yourself to the rather different action.

When the great day dawns that gives you your baptism in salmon fishing it is advisable, if possible, to get some friend or even a hired man to go to the river with you and start you off.

You will probably be able to pick out for yourself the more obvious pools. But there will be many which are not easily seen, and there will be a lot of water which may look ideal but which has never been known to hold a salmon. Of course, if you are fortunate enough to have hired a beat for a period, you will have a gillie with you and he will be your mentor. But I am writing now more for the man whose salmon fishing is likely to be on one of the many " free " or " ticket " waters, and where local knowledge is of such vast importance.

Having found the pool in which you are going to start and having put up your rod, chosen a suitable fly, donned your waders, you now step into the river—very carefully for the waters are swift and coloured—and start fishing.

The object is to cast your fly out at an angle to the stream and to let it swing round in an arc, covering the strip of river where the fish are lying, until it lies immediately below you. Then you take a couple of steps forward (downstream) and repeat the operation. In this way you work your way down the length of the pool and cover the whole of the water within your reach.

The angle at which you cast will be determined largely by the pace of the current at the particular point you are fishing at the moment. If it is very strong you will have to cast more downstream; if rather slow, then you can afford to cast more squarely across. The general idea is to keep your fly moving at a fairly even pace and, if possible, at a natural angle to the stream. By this I mean that the fly should swim pointing in the same direction as a fish crossing the stream at the same pace would naturally swim. If you allow a big belly to get on to your line the fly will not do this, but will be dragged sideways through the water in an unnatural manner. It is really a problem of navigation. If you row a boat, so that it crosses the river at five miles per hour, to a point directly opposite you on the other bank across a stream flowing at five miles per hour, then you must point the boat at an angle of 45 degrees upstream. Similarly, a fish swimming on the same line and at the same speed must point upstream at an angle of 45 degrees. So, too, must your fly if it is to appear natural.

If, however, you allow a big belly in your line the fly gets dragged across pointing almost directly at your own bank instead of upstream and the whole illusion of a fish swimming is lost.

To avoid belly, therefore, you cast more downstream in a strong current than in a slow one. You should also acquire the habit of " mending " your line (as described on page 144) in most places almost as soon as you have finished your cast, for with a heavy line which sinks readily you will not be able to do so when it is fishing.

In the early spring salmon tend to lie rather on the edges of the strong streams and in deeper and slacker water. The chances are that it is as your fly swings out of the stream and into the easier water at its edge that you will get your first pull.

Salmon take the sunk fly in a variety of ways. Sometimes you will feel a heavy, sudden tug on the line, at others a quiet but firm draw, at others, again, your fly may simply be stopped in its progress and no tightening of the line felt for several seconds. Sometimes a little tiny pluck is felt, occasionally to be repeated. On the occasion when a fish takes at the very end of the cast when the fly is hanging directly below you, nothing may be known until the rod is raised for the next cast. Then it is suddenly realised that a fish is attached.

In whichever way the salmon takes you there is one golden rule—never, never attempt to strike. Indeed, if you are in sufficient control of your nerves and reflexes, do the very opposite. Drop your rod point and give him a moment or two before regaining contact.

The reason for this is not obvious at first. It is that the salmon " takes " in an entirely different manner to the trout. He swims forward and upward to the fly and, taking it in his mouth as it crosses in front of him, continues forward and downward with it, turning at the same time toward a point upstream of his original lie.

Now the moment that he feels the hardness of the hook in his mouth he very naturally opens his mouth and tries to let go of it. Fortunately he has no mechanism for " spitting " so he cannot eject it, and since he is still swimming forward there is no way he can get rid of it unless you, the angler, kindly do this for him by pulling the line, or striking.

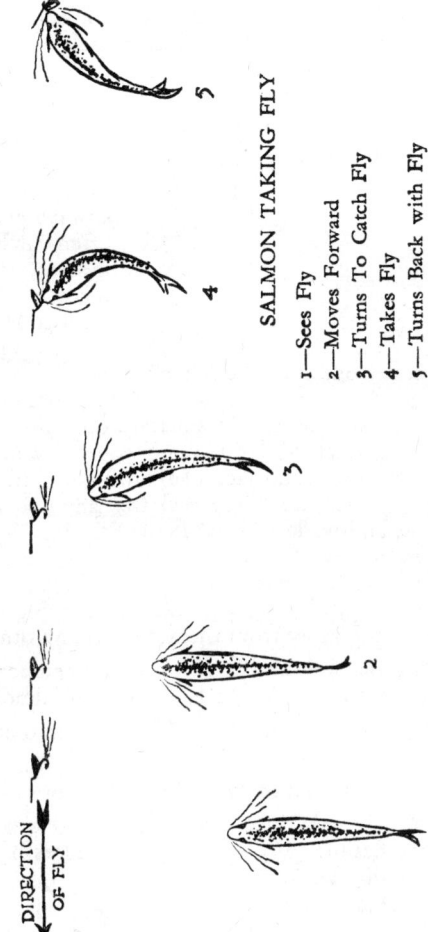

What you want to do is to let the line slacken so that as the fish moves forward and the current sweeps down past him it carries with it a loop of slack line. Now when the fish opens his mouth the fly is carried back *into* his mouth and is only drawn out over the angle of his jaw. Thus :

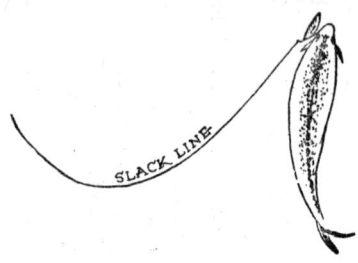

Now there is no escape. Whatever he does he is hooked.

It is for this reason that so many bad casts so often catch fish. The line is slack, and when the fish takes nothing at all is felt until it is too late to do any harm in striking !

Number one rule, then, is never strike. Number two is, as soon as you have hooked a fish, get out of the river and on to the bank, and as nearly squarely opposite him as you can before starting to play him. If you are wading deep or far out, turn round and face your own bank, put your rod over your shoulder, leave the reel free and the fish to his own devices, and wade ashore. If the fish runs now never worry, let him go. Do not attempt to make contact with him until your are on terra firma and level with him. More fish are lost by people standing in the water and trying to play a strong fish running away from them than in any other way.

When playing the fish, if you will remember five things, you will have no difficulty in landing your salmon :

(*i*) Keep always as nearly opposite him as you can.

(*ii*) If he pulls and runs away from you, do not pull back at him, but let him go until he stops—then pull him.

(*iii*) Always keep as much of your line clear of the water as possible. If often pays to stand as high on a bank as you can get.

(*iv*) If the fish bores down and across a strong current and then runs up the other side of it and thereby drowns your line, the weight of water on the line alone will " break " you if you do not let go of everything and allow an absolutely free-running reel while the fish is still moving. You have 100 yards of line and backing and no fish can run that far. Eventually he will stop and the weight of the current on the drowned line will pull him back. Not until you feel the pressure slacken as the fish falls back can you attempt to recover line.

(v) Never attempt, when by yourself, to gaff a fish until it is absolutely still and lying on its side.

Numbers of fish are lost each year by people who miss them with the gaff but catch and break the cast with it. This is inexcusable, and is nearly always the result of trying to gaff a fish still full of fight or of trying to gaff him while he is too deep in the water and still upright.

Where you have a sloping beach try to get the fish into such shallow water that he cannot get upright again. In deep water hold his head into the bank and let him lie quietly on his side for a moment or two before putting the gaff into him. It is generally easier to drive the gaff in over his back and haul him towards you than to put it in below him and try to lift him straight out.

Remember, too, that if the fish does not see you he will be far less frightened. Try, therefore, to keep well away from him until he is on his side. Then his eyes turn down in the sockets and he cannot see.

A few general hints may not be out of place.

Examine your cast and fly frequently. If you think you may have hit the bank always look at your fly, for the barb and hook may be broken. If the cast looks frayed or worn at the knots change or re-tie it. You should always bear in mind that the salmon is an incomparably more powerful fish than any other and that he is of some considerable cash value. By neglecting to see that your tackle is in order you may well lose, not only a splendid trophy, but actually a fish to the value of several pounds sterling.

Always see that the ratchet of your reel is working properly and that nothing has got into the works that may cause a jam. See, too, that neither your line nor your backing has got overrun on the reel. A jamming reel means a certain break if a fish is hooked.

Wading, particularly in rocky pools when the water is coloured, can be unpleasant and dangerous. Some people use a wading stick to feel their way. Provided it is used for this purpose and not for support it is probably very useful. When used for support as a " third leg " it is highly dangerous and will eventually certainly lead to a ducking, or worse. When wading always keep to the lowest path. Wade round obstacles, never over the top of them. And above all never lift one foot unless the other has a firm stance. The dangerous places are those which are not deep but have a swift current and a shingle bed which may roll away under the feet. If you find yourself being swept off your feet, walk straight downstream—even though it may be into deeper water—and as you go edge your way in to your own bank. A wetting through going over the top of your waders is infinitely preferable to the risk of drowning by falling over.

When fishing a pool it is better to go down it with a full yard and a half between casts and then to come back and try again with a different fly, than to restrict your movement to a foot or two between casts. If you do this the fish is apt to see the fly too often before it comes within his reach.

Likewise, if you see a fish rise, do not spend half the morning casting at him. Fish down to him and past him in the ordinary way. Then come back and try him again.

Chapter XX

GREASED-LINE FISHING

When the water warms up, usually in the last fortnight of April, the salmon undergoes a change in his behaviour. Hitherto he has been lying in the deeper parts of the pool and in water with little current. He has been lying resting on the bottom and often behind big boulders and rocks.

When the river reaches a temperature of about 48 degrees, however, the fish start to move into shallower and more streamy water. They tend to lie on top of big rocks rather than behind them. And this allied to the fact that the river is now dropping away to its summer level brings the fish much nearer the surface. The important thing from the angler's point of view is that salmon, which hitherto behaved like deeper water feeding fish, now behave as if they were entirely surface feeders. The signal for this change is, as I have already said, the temperature of the river rising to above 48 degrees.

It follows, therefore, that we must now fish for him in a different way and with rather different tackle.

The first thing to note is that when taking surface flies the salmon evidently mistakes them for something very different to that which he took the sunk fly for. It is, for one thing, much smaller and for a second probably of a less bulky shape. It swims very near the surface and probably not very fast.

We use, as a result, a much smaller fly which is somewhat more sparsely and simply dressed than our early spring flies. Unfortunately, the salmon's preference for size in these greased-line flies appears to be variable within the limits of about a No. 4 to a No. 10. As regards patterns, however, he is not over particular and four patterns are ample. These are chosen on the same principle as those for sunk flies, i.e. " The brighter the day the brighter the fly," etc.

To be completely equipped then we require four patterns each in seven sizes. The patterns I recommend are:

1. Dark fly for dull day—Jenny.
2. Medium fly for normal day—Blue Charm.
3. Bright fly for bright day—Logie.
4. Very bright fly for glaring day—Silver Blue.

Luckily, however, you are never likely to need more than three or four sizes on any one day. The rules which govern the size of flies are as follows:

1. When the water is cool (i.e. 48 degrees to 53 degrees) your basic size will be a No. 5.
2. Water at 53–56.　　Basic size No. 6.
3. 　,,　　56–59.　　　　,,　　,,　　7.
4. 　,,　　59–63.　　　　,,　　,,　　8.
5. 　,,　　63–66.　　　　,,　　,,　　9.
6. 　,,　　above 66.　　 ,,　　,,　　10.

By basic size I mean that this is the size you would use in water flowing at normal speed and neither very shallow nor very deep.

You should vary from your basic size as follows:

(a) When water is very fast and rough—2 sizes bigger.
(b) 　,,　　,,　　fast and rough—1 size bigger.
(c) 　,,　　,,　　very fast and smooth—basic size.
(d) 　,,　　,,　　fast and smooth—1 size smaller.
(e) 　,,　　,,　　very shallow—1 size smaller.
(f) 　,,　　,,　　very deep—1 size bigger.
(g) 　,,　　,,　　very dirty and big—1 to 2 sizes bigger.
(h) 　,,　　,,　　very clean and low—1 size smaller.

With these two tables of information you have as much guidance as it is possible to give—and it is a great deal more than most experienced salmon anglers possess. It remains only to point out that the size of fly used is entirely dependent upon the type of water being fished at the moment. In other words as you fish down a pool the type of water will probably vary from the " very rough, very fast " in the neck to " rough and fast " a little lower down. Then it will become normal. It may then become " very deep " and as you get into a smooth glide at the tail, become " very shallow " and " very fast and smooth " at the same time. If your basic size for the temperature happens to be a No. 7 you will have to start with a No. 5, change down to No. 6, then a No. 7, back again to a No. 6 in the deep bit, returning again to a No. 7 as you pass it and on to a No. 8 and perhaps even a No. 9 in the glide.

This example is perhaps an exaggeration of what you will, in fact, do. But it serves well as an illustration of the principle of the theory of modern greased-line fishing.

Since you are going to fish a fly seldom bigger than one inch in length and often little bigger than a trout fly, it follows that all your tackle must be modified. Your cast, since we are starting at that end, must be fine, as fine as you dare fish with. I would suggest that nothing heavier than .015 inch in diameter, what is technically known as "Padron" and is popularly called "fine salmon" should be used. The cast should be at least three yards in length.

The line, too, must be lighter than for sunk fly-fishing. It must float when greased, and it must float properly even in rough water. A No. 5 "Kingfisher" is the heaviest that has this virtue. A No. 4 floats better, but is too light for all save very small rods.

A small fly requires a fine cast which demands a light line. This in turn needs a smaller rod. In point of fact, a thirteen foot six inch rod is quite suitable for greased-line fishing with a No. 5 line. A twelve foot or twelve foot six inch rod is better especially if used with a No. 4 line. If, however, you are the possessor only of a heavy salmon rod, provided it is not too big, you should be able to get along all right.

Good grease carefully spread on the line is essential. I know of none better than "Mucilin". When "greasing" the line be very careful to see that none gets on to the cast or fly.

When fishing for so powerful a fish with such fine tackle it is essential that your reel should:

(a) hold sufficient backing—at least eighty yards.
(b) be very light in the ratchet or check.

Apart from this, provided it balances the rod, one reel seems to me as good as another.

There are not many rivers which, by the time greased-line fishing starts, have not fallen to a level where wading is, if not imperative, at least such an advantage as to be almost obligatory. And it is fairly true to say that it should be the angler's first concern to get into the water as soon as possible. Do not be put off by people telling you "This pool can perfectly well be fished from the bank". It hardly ever can: and the reason is that as a general principle when fishing the small fly your object should be to fish it over the lies as slowly as you possibly can. The nearer you are to the axis of these lies the more slowly can you bring the fly over them.

There is an unfortunate misconception due entirely to the misinterpretation of Mr. Arthur Wood's (the "inventor" of this method) words. This is that you should cast very square across the stream—even upstream—and allow your fly to fish round, as a result, very fast. This is completely wrong and is fatal to success. With the greased line the more slowly you can fish the fly—the longer you can make it take to swing round from the angle at which you cast it to a line directly below you, the greater your chances of catching fish.

Consequently every artifice, every wile that you possess, should be directed to this end. The first is your power of wading. The nearer you can get to where the fish are lying, the more downstream you can afford to cast while still covering the fish. You will doubtless be told that by wading deep you are frightening the salmon. Nonsense! The only fish you can frighten are those you have already fished over and which have not taken: and you will only temporarily disturb these if you wade right into their lies. They will be back again before you have gone twenty feet past them.

The second trick you can use to keep the fly moving slowly is "mending" the line, which we have already described (page 144). Do not be afraid to mend and overmend your line as often as you like during the fishing of a cast. Above all you must keep a downstream belly out of your line, for such a belly means a fast moving fly axiomatically.

As with the sunk line so, too, with the greased line, when fishing down a pool be careful to take a *full* yard and a half (two yards is better) between casts, and do not cast too often over a fish you have seen show himself.

As you fish down you will be watching the surface of the water about where your fly is. If a fish comes at you you will probably see him rise rather like a big trout long before you feel anything on the line. When you see such a rise you must do *absolutely nothing*. Above all you must not attempt to strike. The fish must be allowed to take the fly in his mouth, go down with it and turn away. This all takes a second or two, sometimes more, and not until he has done this and has himself tightened up on your line dare you raise the rod to gain contact. Some people, myself included, actually pull off a yard of line from the reel and leave it free for the fish to take away so as to give him longer before he tightens up. For the beginner this is perhaps too stiff a test. But strike *he must not*. Never, never, never.

Chapter XXI

SPINNING FOR SALMON

THERE is a tendency to-day towards more and more spinning and less and less fly-fishing for salmon. This is an unqualified tragedy. And I say this not in any spirit of derogation—for there is much art and skill in spinning—but because the motives which have led to this state of affairs refute the true spirit of angling. Spinning is displacing fly-fishing because it is an easier way for those who want a big bag regardless of how they get it to achieve their object. Many who like to boast of their successes but who will not trouble to achieve proficiency in fly-fishing find that with modern " foolproof " tackle the catching of salmon in well-stocked waters is a comparatively simple matter with a spinning-rod. These are not fishermen. They have not learnt the first and fundamental principle of angling proper; that it is not what you catch but the way that you catch it that gives the spiritual satisfaction, that is the whole reason for fishing at all. And if you do not agree with this then your proper weapon is not a rod and line but a drag-net.

Do not suppose, however, that in spinning you have the magic key which opens the door to certain success. Do not suppose either that by confining yourself to spinning you will catch more than by fly-fishing. You will not. In the long run the competent fly-fisherman will always beat the spinning expert. The truth is that the incompetent angler can catch a few fish with the spinning-rod; with the fly-rod he will catch practically nothing.

There are certain conditions where spinning will usually beat fly-fishing, occasionally when it offers the only possible chance of catching a fish. It should in my humble opinion be confined to such conditions.

The fly is at a disadvantage :

1. In very slow-moving water such as the deep, still pools in the Wye or some of the southern rivers.

2. In a river much swollen with flood water.
3. In very dirty water.

For spinning you will require a special set of equipment. Of these there are two usual types whose cost is much about the same in either case and the choice of which is a matter for individual preference. The first is a rod of between nine and twelve feet in length with a reel carrying a comparatively heavy line. The second is a rod of six to eight feet in length with a reel carrying a "thread-line". The first might be called the normal equipment, but the second is becoming more popular every season.

The rod for the normal method should be specially constructed either of split-cane or of greenheart, and should be powerful enough to hold a heavy fish in strong water. The rings should be porcelain or agate-lined throughout and the ring nearest the reel should be of large diameter.

The reel may be one of two types, the revolving-drum or the stationary-drum type. The first is nowadays the most usual.

The simplest form of such reels is the free-running "Nottingham" reel (Illustration No. 9). In the hands of an expert no better casting reel has ever been devised. It has the virtue of simplicity and cheapness, but it requires much practice to use it properly. This has been modified by various tackle-makers, with the intention of producing an article which is less liable to over-

runs and tangles in the hands of the inexperienced. Messrs. Hardy's Silex range is probably the best known of these and these reels are delightfully simple and trouble-free in use.

In casting with any form of revolving-drum reel and "normal" line, the bait is wound up until the cast is almost at the top ring, and the rod is then swung back slowly until it is roughly parallel to the bank and pointing upstream, when it is rapidly swung forward and slightly upwards through an angle of about 180 degrees. The bait now pulls the line off the reel and flies out in an arc through the air to land in the water at an angle of roughly 45 degrees downstream. Except with a "Nottingham" very little practice is required to achieve proficiency in casting with these reels.

The fixed-spool type of reel for "normal" bait-fishing is seldom seen nowadays. The "Malloch" reel exemplifies this. The reel appears to be of the revolving-drum type at first glance, and is used as such in every operation except casting. When about to cast the drum is turned through a right-angle and now lies square to the axis of the rod; and as the cast is made the line is pulled off the ride of the drum in coils. It is easy to use, but has limitations in the distance it will cast and in the fact that, like all fixed-spool reels, it puts a twist into the line when casting.

The rod for thread-line fishing is essentially much lighter and less powerful than that required for "normal" spinning. Usually they are of split-cane, but to-day excellent tubular steel rods are being made for this purpose. They seldom exceed eight feet in length. Very often they are made with detachable handles, besides being in two pieces. This makes for a very neat and handy package when taken down for travelling.

Thread-line reels also fall into two classes: those with fixed spools and those with revolving drums. The former are the originals and are exemplified by the "Illingworth" and by Messrs. Hardy's Altex (see page 157 for illustration). These are simple to use and perfectly satisfactory, but for the fact that the line gets twisted and consequently requires replacement and much attention at frequent intervals.

Revolving-drum thread-line reels are miracles of precision manufacture and are so simple to use and so trouble-free that they will almost certainly eventually displace all other forms of spinning reel. The Pfleuger, an American reel, is probably the best known; but reels of the same type have now been manufactured under many different names in this country.

The great advantage that these reels have lies in the ability which they bestow upon their user to cast very light baits long distances without either effort or the fear of over-runs. They have a geared wind-in mechanism which allows the bait to be recovered quickly and, often an adjustable friction clutch, which allows the angler who has hooked a fish to set the clutch to slip at something less than the breaking-strain of the line and to continue winding in quite regardless of what the fish is doing.

Whether you use a nylon, dressed silk or an undressed line on a thread-line reel is entirely a matter of personal preference. I do not care for nylon on the whole as it is somewhat springy on the reel and sometimes does not run off freely. Silk lines have the disadvantage of tightening on the drum when they get wet and not running freely for a few casts at the start.

The breaking-strain should, for salmon, be not less than seven pounds if you want to have any control whatsoever over a hooked fish.

Spinning, as I have indicated, is essentially a method which should be used when the chances of success with a fly are remote. Such occasions are usually in the early season, or in spates in the summer and autumn. They are, nine times out of ten, to be found only in a river that is bigger than its normal. Low water spinning is a totally different method and one which we shall discuss later.

The trace or cast which you require should either be of gut of fair thickness or of piano wire. It should contain at least two swivels (the box-type are the best) and it is best to have it looped at both ends.

Of baits there are many types. They fall into two main categories—the spinning baits and the wobbling baits.

The former divide themselves into two families: the natural and the artificial. Of the natural the most popular are the sand-eel tail, the sprat, the gudgeon, and the loach. All of these are usually mounted on one of the many types of tackle which have (*a*) a mouth-lead which is inserted into the bait, (*b*) a flight of one or more treble hooks fixed to the tackle by stout gut. The illustration (No. 10) shows three types and is self-explanatory.

Artificial spinning baits are legion. The most popular, without doubt, are " Devon Minnows ". These may be either plain silver or gold, or they may be painted half-blue, half-silver or gold, or half-brown and half-gold. The best salmon sizes lie between three to four inches. Commonly used, too, are natural baits, especially golden sprats, dipped in clear plastic solution which preserves them immune to destruction in the ordinary wear and tear of fishing.

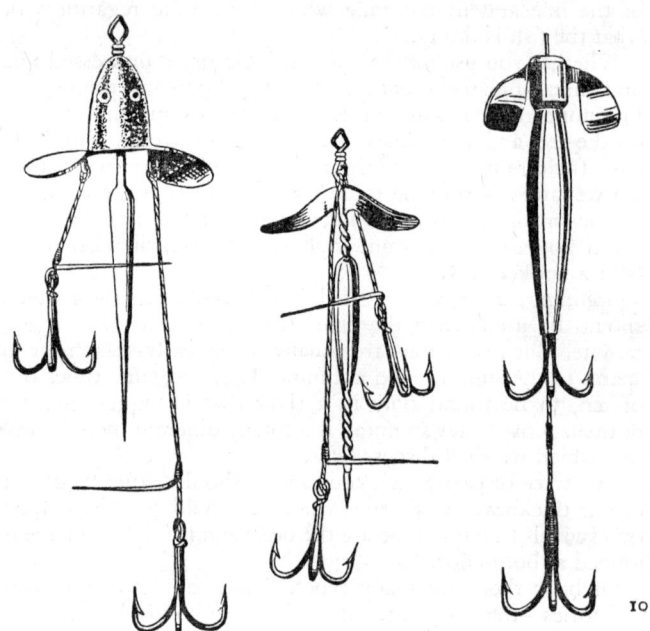

10

Spoons form a good lure in very dirty water. These are made in a variety of shapes, some are all gold or all silver; others gold or copper on one side and silver on the other.

Other popular baits are the " phantom minnow ", the wagtail and the reflex minnow, and gaining increasingly in modern use, the American " plug " baits.

In the conditions which we are considering the object of using bait rather than fly is generally that it can be fished more deeply than can the fly, and can be kept in motion more easily in still water. You will require, therefore, a lead attached to your cast or trace. Either the spiral lead or an anti-kink lead will fill the bill, and it should be of such size that when winding-in slowly the bait fishes as deeply as is reasonable without touching the bottom. In normal salmon rivers the combined weight of bait and lead will be in the region of two and a half ounces.

Most of your spinning will be done from the bank, though occasionally you may need to wade, and sometimes fish out of a boat. The method of fishing a pool is precisely the same as when fly-fishing. You should start at the top of the pool and work your way down it, leaving an interval of perhaps two and a half yards between casts. If you cast accurately at the same angle each time, and wind in at the same speed, you will thus cover the whole of your water and give every fish a chance of taking your bait.

In boat-fishing in very still pools, you should preferably anchor the boat and imagining yourself as the centre, cast all round the clock and try to vary the speed of winding-in from cast to cast. You may thus have from twenty to thirty casts from the same spot. Then move the boat and repeat the process.

You will inevitably at some time or another get foul on the bottom when spinning. This accident is aggravated by the tendency to strike immediately anything is felt to touch the bait.

The first thing to do on getting " hooked-up " is to pull a yard or two of line off the reel and pay it out downstream. Then give the rod a sharp jerk and the bait may free itself. If this fails, walk downstream as far as is practicable and get below the obstruction. Now give a good hard pull. If this does not succeed go back upstream as far as you can and repeat the process.

When all else fails you should try an otter of some sort (Illustration No. 11). The illustration shows the construction of a simple wooden one. A bottle (corked) with a string tied round the neck and a chicken-ring attached to the string does nearly as well. Slip the chicken-ring over the line and allow the otter or bottle to slide down the line and to float beyond the obstruction. When it has reached a position downstream of where you judge your bait to be hold the line firm for a minute or so while the otter " swims " to a point outside your bait. Then freeing it for a second, pull it as hard as you dare. By transmitting the direction of your pull to that in which the bait struck the obstruction, this will in most cases suffice to free it. If it fails you are going to have to

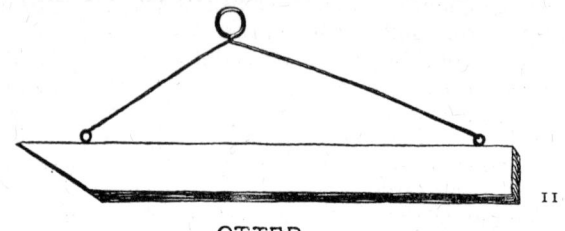

OTTER

break and lose your bait. Don't throw away the otter, too, as I see a good many people doing. Walk downstream and allow the otter to swim back to you along the line.

Low-water spinning demands a special technique and the use of a different size of bait. Just as in summer fly-fishing the small greased-line flies take the place of the big sunk flies, so a much smaller spinning bait is used in low, warm water; and it is fished as nearly as possible to the surface.

Small light baits are difficult to cast. The " normal " type of spinning-rod and reel is not generally capable of dealing with summer baits. The thread-line outfits, however, especially the single-handed Pfleuger type equipments, are ideal.

The bait should be between one to two inches in length and of between half and one ounce in weight. It may either be a natural bait, such as a minnow or a small loach or gudgeon, or an artificial, such as a Devon or a small spoon. It is cast in the normal manner, but when fishing it the reel should be wound in much faster. Nor should the angler confine himself to casting at an angle downstream. Cast square across and even upstream from time to time and reel in quickly enough not to get snagged. This form of fishing can be very deadly indeed, particularly when the river has nearly fallen back after a small rise.

A bait which has always found much favour with salmon fishermen and which can, at times, appear irresistible to the fish and at others, give every evidence of scaring them right out of any not very deep pool is the prawn.

The best prawns for bait are fresh-boiled ones which may either be used on the day of preparation or be preserved in salt for up to a fortnight. Prawns bottled in formalin do not keep a natural colour and it is possible that the smell of the preservative may be unattractive to the fish.

Prawns are mounted on a special tackle and are either spun or fished by the " sink and draw " method.

If spinning is preferred, and in most instances it is to be advised, unless you are with an expert in the other method, it is best to mount the prawn on a plain bar with the hook flights attached to its eye. I prefer the mount to be without spinners, but to attach the bait with a piece of piano wire to a spinner about half-way up the trace. This allows the prawn to swim at a more natural angle.

The prawn is essentially the bait for low, clear water. When the fish want it they will grab at it almost as soon as it hits the surface. In July and August very big bags can sometimes be made in our well-stocked northern rivers with the prawn. But equally there are certain days when they will not take it. And on such an occasion it is probably fatal to your own and everyone else's fishing to persevere with it. When salmon do not want it, there is no doubt whatever that they are desperately frightened by a prawn.

Fishing a prawn can be a most amusing pastime for an odd occasion. Personally, I would ban its use from all salmon rivers because of its effect on other people's chances. But, nevertheless, I must agree that in low, clear water it is fascinating to watch the progress of your prawn through a pool, followed often by two or three shadowy shapes at once. To fish your prawn up to the end of the cast and to watch a fish rush forward just as you are lifting it out of the water is as exciting as anything I know in fishing. But if you have the general good of the sport, and particularly if you have other anglers sharing your beat, keep the prawn for special occasions. Do not make a habit of it.

Great sport can be had, too, by shrimping for salmon in the fast stickles and small pools in summer-time. Since this technique is identical with that described in the same method of trout fishing I would refer you to Chapter XVIII for a description of it.

If you spin much in water when there is a big stock of fish it is inevitable that you will sooner or later foul-hook a fish. The most normal place to do this is either in the back fin or in the tail. For some time you will not realise that your fish is not hooked in the mouth; but any salmon that takes an unusually long time to show signs of tiring should be suspected of being foul-hooked. Of course it may be a whale!

A fish hooked in the tail is, once you know you have got him there, fairly easy to deal with. Keep pulling him from upstream. The one thing he is really frightened of is being held with his head downstream in the current, for then he cannot breathe. If you do this his efforts to get turned right way round will soon tire him out.

The fish hooked in the middle of the back is not so easy. Your bait has hold of him at about his point of balance, and your best chance usually lies in making him fight his way upstream against the drag of the line in the current. In this case, therefore, go downstream and pull him. He will try to resist and go the other way. When gaffing a foul-hooked fish it is doubly important to remember to keep the gaff clear of the trace and hooks.

Chapter XXII

WORMING FOR SALMON

FLY-FISHING stands alone as an artistic and satisfying method of catching salmon. Second, and far above spinning in my humble opinion, stands worm-fishing.

The worm is essentially that bait which only succeeds when the fly is impossible. It is primarily the lure for very dirty water. It is not, as a rule, until the last of the snow has gone in May that the worm can be used in Scotch salmon rivers. Until then any " spate " is usually of clean, melted snow. When the river is so coloured that you cannot see your fingers when you put your hand in it, and when it is clearing up after such a spate, then is the time to try the worm.

The tackle is simple. Use your fly-rod, and attach a stout gut cast of not more than one foot in length. To this tie a single " hook to gut " of large size. On this hook thread at least half a dozen good-sized, well-scoured worms. You require no lead since any weight deprives you of the delicacy of touch which is necessary.

You must forget all about the pools if the water is really big. You want to fish in the quiet eddies along the bank wherever the water is about four feet or more in depth. Here you throw your worm in upstream and, with a few feet of line pulled off your reel, let it bump quietly down over the bottom until it either gets washed on to the shore or stuck behind a stone. If the bank is clear it is best to walk downstream for a few yards with it. Then you can by gently lifting it over obstructions keep it moving for quite long swims. Each length of river thus fished should be gone over again once or twice with the bait cast at different distances from the shore. Particularly good spots are the inside curves of pools which have a shelving bottom and a wide stretch of calm water even in the biggest spates. Little bays into which the sand washes are also good places, and any grass bank going fairly steeply down to the river's edge at normal heights is worth a trial.

The salmon will, as a rule, do little more than stop your bait, but when he first takes it you will then feel a very gentle " mouthing " at your worms, much more restrained than the " tit-tit " of a trout. If you now tighten up very slightly you will feel the fish move an inch or two away with the bait as if he were frightened of someone trying to rob him of it.

You must now, having identified the reason for your bait stopping as a fish, keep but the most gentle of contacts with him. Any sudden jerk or pull will frighten him away.

After what seems an age, actually probably not more than ten to fifteen seconds, you will see the line move off quite fast. Count five for luck and then strike. The chances are that you will have him.

Worm-fishing is a most difficult art, firstly, because only experience can really teach you in a river in spate which are the best places to fish, and secondly, because few beginners can sustain the excitement of knowing that a salmon has hold of their bait without immediately striking and pulling the hooks away before he has had time to make off with it.

It is always best to respect local knowledge and to ask and take advice as to where your best chances lie in fishing the worm in an unknown river. If you are fishing in the right place and in suitable conditions you will have a thrilling day. Remember always to keep your hook baited with fresh, lively worms and to give any fish which takes you much more time than you think is reasonable before you strike.

Upstream worm-fishing in low water is, once more, precisely the same technique as that used in trout fishing. The only differences lie in the fact that your hook should be bigger and should be baited with two fair-sized worms or one very big one and that you will be fishing in somewhat deeper water.

This method is suitable only in smaller rivers, or rivers in which you can wade virtually all over them at low water.

The type of place to choose is not a salmon pool, but those rapids between pools and which have big, exposed rocks dotted about in them. These are places not usually fished either by fly-anglers or by those spinning. Consequently, in association waters, the upstream wormer often has them to himself. And it is surprising in warm weather what a number of salmon choose to lie in such places.

The technique, as I have said, is the same as that for trout fishing—but it is all on a somewhat larger and stronger scale. Wading is usually absolutely essential, and it requires both skill and strength to wade up against the strong streams you will encounter. It demands accuracy and practice, too, to be able to lob your worms under-hand into the eddies and backwaters which are found behind each big stone and rock. And as ever with the worm, it requires the highest measure of self-discipline and control to allow a fish which is interested to the extent of toying with your bait the time in which to take it properly. A fascinating pastime.

Chapter XXIII

SEA-TROUT FISHING

THE opportunities of catching sea-trout, possibly the most sporting of all the game fish in these islands, are almost limitless to the angler keen enough to seek out his sport in the lesser-known by-ways. In the south of England most of the sea-trout fishing is in strictly preserved waters with fabulous rentals, but in the West Country a certain amount of free or ticket fishing may be had. But on the west coast, in Wales, and in the Lake District, good sea-trout fishing can often be obtained for the asking, while virtually the whole of the west coast of Scotland offers limitless opportunities of free fishing, both in small lochs and in their outflows to the sea. In the Northern Islands and in the bays on the north coast of Scotland, some of the most fascinating of all forms of fishing for sea-trout may be indulged in free of cost by anyone, fly-fishing or worming in the sea itself. Throughout Scotland, and in many parts of England, excellent sea-trout fishing can be had in the tidal water of the estuaries of many of our salmon rivers. This, too, in most cases is either free or nearly so.

Nothing special need be said about the technique of sea-trout fishing. In every case it is identical with either that of brown trout fishing or occasionally of salmon fishing. A general-purpose trout rod with its normal line and reel will usually suffice, though it may be advisable to use a slightly stronger cast. The flies will be of a different type and will vary according to the time and place where you are fishing.

Sea-trout fishing falls into three categories : loch fishing, river fishing and sea or estuary fishing. Let us look at them each in turn.

Loch fishing is easy. Except that you should use slightly larger flies as a general rule, and that you should remember that sea-trout are much softer in the mouth than brown trout, the system of fishing for the former is identical in every respect with that of brown trout fishing. If you will turn to Chapter XV on loch fishing for brown trout you will find all that it is necessary to know. For flies you should rely largely on local knowledge, since for some reason or another sea-trout definitely take certain patterns better than others in every district.

It is probable, however, that with a Butcher, a Cinnamon and Silver, and a Grouse and Claret, you will have three standard patterns which, failing the assistance of local advice, will catch these fish in most places.

One possible difference between sea-trout and brown trout fishing in lochs lies in the times of day which are most successful. Generally speaking sea-trout do not care for a bright light and feed most freely before the sun is up in the morning and at dusk in the evening. Often the middle of the day in summertime is quite hopeless.

River fishing for sea-trout is possibly more akin to greased-line fishing for salmon than trout fishing. They can perfectly well be caught on a trout rod and with trout tackle. But, in east coast rivers especially, the average weight of the fish you will catch is liable to be high. In one Scottish river which I fish it is, for instance, over three pounds, and sea-trout of between seven to ten pounds are common. In a strong river these big sea-trout will succeed in breaking you more often than not with trout tackle, and I would strongly advise the use of a twelve-foot rod wherever such sizes of fish are likely to be encountered.

The fly should, generally speaking, be of the same pattern as that used for salmon fishing. No better sea-trout flies for river fishing have ever been tied than the Blue Charm and the Silver Blue. And these flies should be fished singly down the pool in exactly the same manner as if greased-line fishing for salmon.

The late evening, just as darkness is falling is, if conditions are right, the great moment for hooking the big sea-trout. The conditions required are preferably a moonless evening and one in which no mist rises from the surface of the water. You may be fishing what appears to be a dead river the whole of the early evening. But as it begins to darken and when the colour fades from the sky the surface of the pool begins to come to life with the rings and splashes of big sea-trout starting to feed. The tendency now is for the fish to fall back out of the deeper parts of the pool into the shallow glides at the tail. And here, on a good evening, you may hook half a dozen or more in that magic hour between twilight and darkness.

It is advisable, as a rule, once it begins to get really dark, to take up your station in the tail of some likely pool and to stay there throughout the evening rise. Sea-trout do not, like salmon, remain in one lie. They tend rather to cruise about in shoals at this time of the evening, and you will fish more easily and with perhaps better chances of success if you remain in the one stance rather than move about.

Sea-trout, especially those caught on a summer evening while still fresh run, pull and fight in a manner equalled by no other fish of their weight. A seven-pound sea-trout will give twice the play of a salmon of the same size. Moreover, he will leap repeatedly from the water and may easily take out seventy to eighty yards of line and backing in a single rush across and upstream. This is, indeed, the king of our sporting fish. If ever you can get a June night's fishing on such a river as the Spey you will be able to say to yourself that you have experienced the greatest thrill and joy that can befall a fisherman.

Possibly the opportunities of estuary fishing are more easily available than even loch fishing. In many localities all fishing below high-water mark is free to all, and at the mouths of many of our rivers the local town has fishing rights in the estuary and sometimes in the bottom pools which are available to visitors at very small charge.

Much estuary fishing is done from boats, and advantage is taken of the fact that sea-trout follow the shoals of young herring and sprats into the estuaries and gorge themselves on this food. Trolling is consequently the normal custom, and if you are content to sit in a boat and be rowed, or row it about with your line hanging over the stern, this is not a bad way of catching sea-trout. You should not, however, use your good fly-line for this purpose, since the salt water will quickly ruin it. Use preferably an undressed line and, where possible a sea reel, and wash both carefully in fresh water after each day's fishing.

But if you want the best of estuary fishing, do not be tempted into a boat. Rather choose some point where the estuary narrows and where both on the ebb and flow there is a good stream running with the tide, put on a pair of waders and remain roughly in the same spot. Now you fish just as if in a river, casting your fly and letting it swing round in the stream. From about three hours before high tide, and for about three hours after the ebb has started, i.e. about three hours on either side of high tide with about an hour off during the slack water in the middle, your chances are good.

The flies you require are very different from those needed for river fishing. They must represent the young herring or the sand-eel, and are usually known as terrors (Illustration

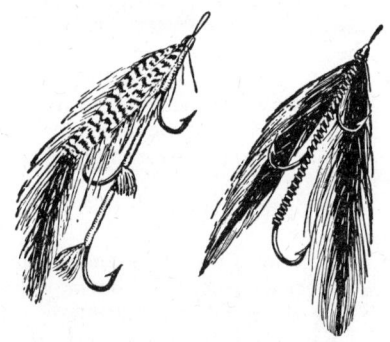

TERRORS

12

No. 12). They are made in a variety of colours, but are generally between two to three inches in length. The illustration shows their construction. Usually with a blue, a red and a grey one you are completely equipped. The blue represents the herring, the grey probably the sand-eel. The red one may be taken for either, or form of crustacean. Often you can see the little herrings leaping out of the water from their shoals as the sea-trout go for them. When such a shoal passes you keep your fly in the water and fish " hard ". Sometimes, too, you may locate the progress of a shoal by watching the terns diving on them. This form of fishing is full of interest. You will see great trout rolling over on the surface as they move into or out of the estuary. They seldom take when doing this. Occasionally you will see a salmon jump—he never seems to take—or a seal looking for all the world like a labrador dog, following a shoal of troat. It is above all in the estuaries where the observant fisherman can learn about the movement of his fish by watching the behaviour of the other creatures which inhabit it.

As a change from fly-fishing, many like to spin for sea-trout in the estuaries. I do not think it is necessary to say any more about this than that the method of doing so is precisely the same as for brown trout, and that the bait should be either a small sand-eel or a sprat, or alternatively a Devon minnow or a spoon. Again, remember that the utmost care must be taken in washing your line and reel after the day's fishing. Moth and rust cannot compare for corruption with salt water.

Sea-trout also take the worm readily under the same conditions which salmon take it in a river. And they should be fished for in precisely the same manner and with the same tackle and bait. Chapter XXII gives all the necessary information. I need only add that if you are fortunate enough to strike a really dirty spate on a good sea-trout river in July or August you may easily catch twenty or thirty fish in an hour or two's fishing!

In a loch sea-trout sometimes will take the worm very readily. This is more especially true of the lochs which are more or less brackish and which fill with salt water at every spring tide. Here the worm is fished in exactly the same method as for brown trout and this is described in Chapter XV. It may be of interest to know that the record sea-trout for these islands, twenty-nine pounds, was caught in Loch Stennes in the Orkneys by such a method.

Some confusion may arise in your mind over the nomenclature of sea-trout in different parts of the country. It is now recognised that the sea-trout and the brown trout are of precisely the same species, Salmo Trutta, but that the former is of a variety which has acquired or inherited a sea-going habit. There are, in consequence, a vast number of intermediate varieties which can neither be described as proper sea-trout nor as proper brown trout. Often these are known as slob-trout and they are very common in most brackish water.

Sea-trout and slob-trout are known by all sorts of different names. Peel, Sewin, Whitting, Bull-trout, Scruff, Finnoch, Herling and White Trout are but a few of the names given them in different localities.

In the far north and off the islands on the west coast of Scotland a unique form of sea-trout fishing can be enjoyed which is absolutely free to anyone who chooses to take advantage of it. This is fly-fishing or worm-fishing in the sea itself. September and October are generally the best months, for this is essentially fishing for those trout which are coming into tiny burns to spawn and which, as a result, leave their entry into fresh water to the last possible moment. By mid-September the little bays into which these small burns flow will be full of sea-trout waiting for a spate to run up into the fresh water. By wading into the sea and fishing off the weed beds, either with a terror fly (see earlier part of chapter), or with a worm, these fish can be caught, often in great numbers and, fresh from their feeding ground, of a quality and beauty never to be equalled by any other fish. For any angler whose holiday falls rather late in the year no more enjoyable way of spending it can be recommended than of making the long journey northwards and fishing sea-trout in the sea itself.

Chapter XXIV
KNOTS AND ODDMENTS

A few basic knots are an essential part of the stock-in-trade of every angler. The first of these is a knot used for tying on a fly or a looped hook on to a cast. The "figure of 8" is undoubtedly the best and most useful of these.

Hold the eye of loop A in the left hand. Pass the gut B through the eye A from underneath, over the side of the eye and round and under the shank. Take it back over A but under B and pass it now round and under the free end of B and back again through the original loop made by B.

This knot may be used for attaching lines to casts, for tying on flies, or for anything where a fixed loop and a free end are involved.

In making up a spinning trace with swivels it is not, however, advisable to use a "figure of 8" since the small tail of gut lying alongside the swivel may interfere with the proper functioning of the swivel. Use preferably the "Fisherman's Bend".

Pass A through the eye of the swivel B, over and through again. Take end of A and pass through the two bends made round the swivel, B, and now tie a half-hitch and pull tight. Finish off with another half-hitch and tighten.

To make a cast or join two pieces of gut without having ends sticking out there is only one knot which will do. This is the Blood Knot. It is much easier than it looks and the ability to tie this and to make up your own casts will halve your expenditure on these items. The illustration is, I think, self-explanatory.

When the stage shown in the illustration is reached all that remains is to pull the two standing pieces of the cast firmly apart. The knot then runs up together leaving the two ends standing out from the middle at right-angles. These can be cut off level with the knot. Need I add that all gut should be  thoroughly well soaked, at least an hour in tepid water or six hours in cold water, before any attempt is made to tie knots in it.

To make a loop at the end of a cast or trace just make a simple over-hand knot on the gut about six inches from the end.

Then form the required loop and pass the end back through the over-hand knot. Tighten up by pulling the standing part and finish off with a half-hitch made with the "end".

To attach a dropper hook or fly to a cast either:

(a) Cut the cast and rejoin with a blood knot leaving one of the "ends" sufficiently long, say three inches, to tie the fly or hook on to.

(b) Tie the fly on to a separate piece of gut. Make a loop at the end of this gut. Cut the cast and re-tie with a blood knot. Before pulling this tight insert the loop into the centre of the knot, pass the fly through it and tighten. Then tighten the blood knot. Before this last operation the knot will appear thus:

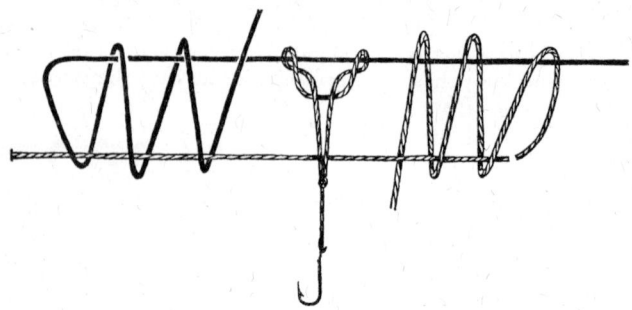

The line should always be spliced, never knotted on to the backing. This is a simple operation if properly done. Dry the line and the backing. Then fray the ends of both for about one-third of an inch. Lay the two ends parallel to and overlapping each other by about an inch. If possible wax the two ends first. Now tie the whipping silk firmly round both ends to be spliced. Do not trim the knot made by the whipping silk but leave the " end " and tuck it in between the line and backing. Whip round the two ends until past the overlap. Then return a second time over the splice. Finish off with a " whip finish " thus:

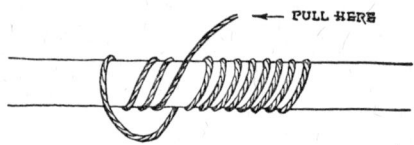

After finishing off the splice, wax and then varnish.

The same technique, i.e. whipping, may be used in mending two pieces of a broken top of a rod.

Hook sizes are measured from the base of the eye to the end of the bend of the hook in a straight line.

Hooks are classified on one of three scales, either by length in inches or by the numbers of the " old scale " (the most usual), or by those of the "new scale". A comparative list is given for reference.

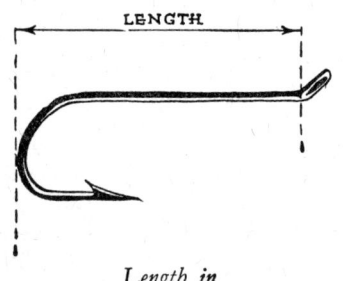

Old Scale	Length *in* Inches	New Scale
	2¾	8/0
	2½	7/0
	2¼	6/0
	2	5/0
	1⅞	4/0
	1¾	3/0
	1⅝	2/0
	1½	1/0
	1⅜	1½
	1¼	1
	1⅛	2
	1	3
	15/16	4
	14/16	5
	13/16	6
9	¾	7
8	11/16	8
7	10/16	9
6	9/16	10
5	½	11
4	7/16	12
3	12/32	13
2	11/32	14
1	10/32	15
0	9/32	16
00	¼	17
000	7/32	18

Chapter XXV

FISHING ETIQUETTE

FISHING is the gentle sport and its followers have, as a result, an inborn sense of consideration for their brother-anglers. In most cases where a breach of the normal rules of behaviour occur it has been, in my experience, due to a lack of understanding on the part of the offender. Only on the famous salmon rivers, where often the tenant anglers have more money than sense, and an idea that because they are rich enough to pay fantastic prices, they need not observe the ordinary standards of civilised manners, have I ever seen wilful and persistent breaches of fishing etiquette.

However keen you are to catch a fish, or to give yourself the best chance of doing so, never forget that " the other fellow " has precisely the same thoughts at the back of his mind; and if he is the first-comer in any particular pool or swim, you should let him have his " go " without in any way interfering with his sport. It is out of consideration for the pleasure of others that all the rules of the etiquette of fishing have grown into being. And if you bear this always in mind it is unlikely that, even as a beginner, you are likely to transgress.

" First come, first served " is a general and very fair rule in all association and club waters. It is also the rule when fishing a river of which you have the rights only of one bank and an " opponent " is fishing opposite you. Always come in behind another fisherman and never in front of him. Likewise, if you see someone else waiting to fish behind you, be sure not to linger unduly over the best bits.

If a fellow fisherman hooks a fish and it is even remotely possible that it may run your way always reel in yourself and give the fortunate angler every chance of landing his prize. You would like him to do the same for you!

Try not to lie about fishing. I do not necessarily mean the little white ones which merely double the weight of your catch. I mean rather that when a brother-angler asks if there are fish in a certain place and you know there are but want it to be left undisturbed for yourself, tell him the truth and rejoice with him rather than envy him if he is successful as a result of the advice you have given him.

Where limits upon the size of fish that may be kept are placed, always observe these faithfully. They are laid down for the benefit of the community generally and not solely for the purpose of depriving you of the results of your skill. By the same token be very gentle and solicitous of the fish you may need to put back. Cool and wet your hand before holding him. Extract the hooks with as little force and damage as possible; and when you put him back don't just throw him in from the bank—he has a very delicate swim bladder which you can easily rupture and kill him; put him gently in the water and if he shows a tendency to turn upside down hold him upright with his head to the stream until he starts to breathe properly. He will then swim away.

Many farmers and riparian owners are good to the fishing fraternity by allowing them access to the river or lake. Do not abuse this hospitality. Shut all gates which were found shut. Keep to paths and don't wander about over growing crops, and don't bully the livestock. Many farmers quite rightly object if their lambing ewes are chased about by irresponsible fishermen.

Never cut or break branches off other people's trees!

Where the boundary to your fishing is marked by a post or a stream never never fish a foot beyond it. More fishing rows are caused by this than you would ever imagine.

When certain limitations are placed on the baits which are permitted, likewise observe them rigidly.

If you are fishing from a boat and you see a bank fisherman or wader in the line of your drift, give him the right of way. You can cover infinitely more water than he can.

It is customary, and good manners, if you are spinning to offer to let a fly fisherman fish down a pool first.

Two golden rules of behaviour apply just as much to fishing as to everyday life. " Do as you would be done by " and if there is doubt as to who is in the right, rather concede the point than make an enemy.

INDEX

Ackroyd Fly, 167
Aerialite reel, 85
Alder fly, 54, 58
Alimentary canal, 9
Archer bait mount, 64
Archer flight of hooks, 51

Bait,
  attachment of, 199
  drift-line fishing (sea), 107
  dry fly-fishing (trout), 149–153
  greased line fly-fishing, 177
  hook bait (coarse fish), 27 *et seq.*
  live bait (pike), 76
  pike, 60 *et seq.*
  salmon fly-fishing, 166
  sea fly-fishing, 104
  shore fishing, 90
  shrimp fishing (trout), 159
  spinning for salmon, 183, 186
    ,,   ,, sea fish, 100
    ,,   ,, trout, 158
  wet fly-fishing (trout), 138
  worm fishing (salmon), 189
    ,,   ,, (trout), 161
Barleycorn weight, 78
Barbel, 38
Bass, 94, 104
Bleak, 33
Blue Charm fly, 176, 193
Bream, 39
  ,, (black), 107
  ,, (red), 108
Bickerdyke flight of hooks, 67
Black gnat, 54
Boat fishing, 107
Butcher fly, 193

Carp, 37, 38
Channel Isles, 98
Chub, fly-fishing, 54 *et seq.*
  ,, habitat, 39, 40, 44
  ,, spinning for, 48
  ,, technique for, 45, 46

Cinnamon and Silver fly, 193
Clipper bait, 63
Coachman fly, 59
Coch-y-bondhu fly, 54
Cod, 111
Colonial reel, 85
Colorado bait, 63
Colour, recognition of, 8
Cornwall (sea-spinning), 100

Dabs, 91
Dace, 33, 56
Deal weight, 88
Deep-water fishing, 33
Devon minnows (artificial bait), 159
Devon style spinning, 52
Dog fish, 109
Drifting (loch trout), 148
Drift-line fishing, 107
Dry fly-fishing, 154
  ,,   ,, technique, 183

Ears, fishes', 5
Eggs, fishes', 9
Eyes, fishes', 8

Farewell Weight, 99
Feeding grounds (coarse fish), 23–26
Fins, 9
Fishing Gazette float, 78
Flat fish, 93
Float fishing, 27
Float-legering, 34 *et seq.*
Flounders, 91
Fly-fishing,
  coarse fish, 54 *et seq.*
  dry fly-fishing, 149, 154
  footwear for, 137, 147
  greased line, 176
  sunk fly-fishing, 167
  wet fly-fishing, 122
Foul hooking, 188
Free-lining (coarse fish), 44

GILLS, 4
Greased-line fishing, 175, 178
Greenwell's Glory fly, 54, 138
Ground-bait,
  coarse fish, 32
  free-lining, 45, 46
  legering, 36, 38
  paternoster, 42
  sea-fish, 98
  spinning, 48
Grouse and Claret fly, 193
Gudgeon, 33

HAKE, 111
Hardy's Altex reel, 182
  ,,   favourite fly, 59
  ,,   Jock Scott Wriggler bait, 61
  ,,   Silex reel, 181

ILLINGWORTH REEL, 182

JARDINE FLIGHT OF HOOKS, 67
Jardine spiral weight, 88
  ,,   weight, 78, 94
Jenny fly, 176

KNOTS, 198

LEA, 30
Ledger paternoster, 34
Lee-Lock bait mount, 64
Legering, 34 *et seq.*
Limerick bend hooks, 87
Live-bait, 76 *et seq.*
Ling, 115
Loch-trout (drifting for), 148
Logic fly, 176

MACKEREL, 104, 105, 109
Mallock reel, 182
March Brown fly, 138
Mar Lodge fly, 167
Mending the line, 144 *et seq.*
Mucilin, 77 *et seq.*
Mullet, 96
Mullins snap tackle, 67
Mumbles tackle, 94, 96

NOSE, fishes', 8
Nottingham reel, 72 *et seq.*

Nottingham style, 29

ORGANS, digestive, 9
Otter, 185

PADRON CAST, 177
Pain, sensation of, 8
Parker, Capt. L. A. (snap tackle), 68
Parr, 165
Paternoster, 40, 77 *et seq.*
Perch,
  bait for, 46
  fly-fishing for, 58
  habits of, 28
  legering for, 37
  paternostering for, 40
  spinning for, 58
Pfleuger reel, 182
Pike,
  fly-fishing for, 58
  paternostering for, 40
  spawning of, 75
  spinning for, 60 *et seq.*
Pincher, Chapman, 4
Playing fish, 140
Pollack,
  habitat, 104
  habits, 109
  spinning for, 100
Pouting, 112

RABOULIN (lip-hook), 78
Red Palmer fly, 58
Replacement of fish, 203
Reproduction of fish, 9
Respiration of fish, 5
Roach,
  fly-fishing for, 57
  methods for, 29–32
  summer ledgering for, 57
Rudd,
  fly-fishing for, 57
  methods for, 47

SALMON,
  fly-fishing tackle for, 166
    ,,   technique, 169
  greased-line fishing, 175
  habits of, 165
  spinning for, 180
  worming for, 189

INDEX

Scales, 10
Scarborough reel, 86
Scarborough sea-fishing, 104
Sedge fly, 59
Sharks, 116
Shooting line, 134
Silver Blue fly, 176, 193
Silver Grey fly, 167
Skate, 115
Smolt, 165
Sneed, 105
Spinning,
  Devon style, 52
  grounds for, 104
  low-water, 186
  pike, 69 *et seq.*
  salmon, 180
  sea-fishing, 48
  sink-and-draw style, 69
  technique of, 185
  thread line style, 69
Spoon bait, 63
Stewart tackle, 161
Swallow-tail bait, 50

TACKLE, 13
  big game, 115, 116
  booms, 92
  carrier, 20
  cast, making up, 199
  containers, 18, 20
  dressing (line), 21
  drift-line fishing (sea), 107, 109
  dry fly-fishing, 150
  fine salmon cast, 177
  floats, 14, 20
  ,, freshwater, 27 *et seq.*
  ,, sea, 93
  fly-fishing, 54
  free-lining, 44, 46
  gaff, 70
  ,, sea, 88
  greased line, 177
  hooks, 14
  ,, classification of, 201
  ,, sea, 86
  keep-net, 20
  legering, 34, 35
  lines, 14
  ,, sea, 86

live bait, 76 *et seq.*
loch fishing, 145
net, landing, 17
paternoster, 40
pike, fly-fishing, 60
plummet, 18
priest, 80
reel, 13
  ,, sea, 85
rod, 13, 22
  ,, sea, 84
salmon fly-fishing, 166, 168
  ,, spinning, 181, 186
  ,, worming, 189
sea-angling, 83
sea-spinning, 102
sliding float, 33
spinning, 51, 72
Stewart tackle, 161
swivels, 88
tope, 116
trace, 51
  ,, making up, 198
  ,, sea, 86
trout-salmon, 129, 135
trout spinning, 157
tunny, 117
weight, 16
  ,, sea (sinker), 88, 91
winder, 18
Taste buds, fishes', 8
Tench, 35, 38
Terrors fly, 195
Thread-line fishing, 69
Thunder and Lightning fly, 167
Tight-lining, 30
Tongue, fishes', 8
Tope, 116
Trolling, 194
Trout, 136
  loch-trout, 147
  nomenclature, 196
  sea-trout, estuary, 194
  ,, loch, 192
  ,, river, 193
  ,, sea, 197
  ,, spinning for, 196
  ,, worming for, 196
  shrimp-fishing, 159
  slob-trout, 197

spinning for, 157
  worming for, 161
Tunny, 117

WAGTAIL BAIT, 63
Watermanship, 143
Wet fly-fishing, 137, 122
Whip-finish, 200

Whiting, 111
Wickham's Fancy fly, 138
Wood, Arthur, 178
Wrasse, 112
Wye, 180

ZULU FLY, 59, 138